Sally K. Johnson
7843 Marquette Street
Dallas, Texas 75225
214 - 676 - 4992

D.C.'s Dirty Politics

D.C.'s Dirty Politics

Ben Shapiro

Creators Publishing
Hermosa Beach, CA

Cover art by Peter Kaminski

CREATORS PUBLISHING
737 3rd St
Hermosa Beach, CA 90254
310-337-7003

ISBN (print): 978-1-945630-93-4
ISBN (ebook): 978-1-945630-93-7

First Edition
Printed in the United States of America
1 3 5 7 9 10 8 6 4 2

A Note From the Publisher

Since 1987, Creators has syndicated many of your favorite columns to newspapers. In this digital age, we are bringing collections of those columns to your fingertips. This will allow you to read and reread your favorite columnists, with your own personal digital archive of their work.
—Creators Publishing

Contents

The Anti-Science Mainstreaming of Mental Illness   1

Why the Image of the Great Economic Leader Is   3
Dangerous

The Left Can't Help Overplaying its Hand   5

The Left's Vagina-Based Politics Demeans Women   7

The Left Won't Stop Threatening Violence Against   9
Trump

Can the Super Bowl Save America?   11

How Presidents Shape Their Administrations   13

What If There's No Plan?   16

Trump Is Winning, and Leftists Are Confused   18

The 5 Stages of a Trump Scandal   20

Are We on the Verge of Violence?   22

Why Does It Feel Like Everything's a Scandal?   24

When Does Trump Become the Establishment?   26

On Human Nature and Mike Pence's Dinner Partners   28

The Insanity of the Left's Child Gender-Confusion   30
Agenda

The Democrats Lose Their S—   32

Are We Really Living in Trump's America   34

The Smug Blind Left Is Trump's Best Friend   36

Racism Is Only Racism If Comes From Groups the Left   38
Hates

Happy Legal Guardian of Unspecified Gender Day!   40

No, You're Not a Bigot If You Only Want to Have Sex   42
With People to Which You Are Attracted

How America Lost Its Head   44

The Unbridgeable Gap Between Left and Right Over   46
Human Evil

Trump Didn't Ruin the Media. Obama Did   48

On 'Muh Prunciples'   50

But Reality Isn't Fair   53

Does Being Presidential Matter Anymore?   55
What If There's No Trump-Putin Conspiracy?   57
Yes, Politics Is Dirty. No, It Isn't As Dirty As You Think   59
It Is
Why the Left Protects Islam   61
Instability Is Not Unpredictability   63
Google's Leftist Goggles Leave Googlers Agog   65
The Group That Got Ignored In Charlottesville   67
President Trump and the Politics of Attitude   69
What Hurricane Harvey Teaches Us About Humanity   71
If Republicans Don't Make a Move, They Deserve to Lose   73
Democrats' Newest Plan: Nationalized Health Care   75
The End of the First Amendment   77
The Strategy of Going Too Far   79
The Power of Good   81
'Raising Awareness' Isn't Helping Much   83
The Delusional Optimism of Both Sides   85
The Swamp Is D.C.   87
What an American Hero Looks Like   89
What Are Our Representatives Supposed to Do?   91
The Sultans of America and Their Harems   93
Bill Clinton Won After All   95
Fiscal Responsibility or Lower Taxes   97
How to Deal With Bullies   99
Does Yes Ever Mean Yes?   101
Time to Defund the United Nations   104
About the Author   106

The Anti-Science
Mainstreaming of Mental Illness

January 4, 2017

On Tuesday, the U.K.'s Daily Mail reported that 23-year-old Anna Teshu of Staten Island, New York, has gone missing. Teshu's 15 minutes of fame began in 2015 when she was featured on the internet because her boyfriend was walking her around on a leash in public. Her boyfriend said: "The collar is like a ring for most couples. They use rings, we have a collar." Teshu reportedly enjoyed spending time in a puppy cage, as well. She explained, "The first time I put on a collar I thought, 'Now I need to find someone for the other end.'"

That same year, she was arrested for animal cruelty after allegedly leaving a dog in a hot car. Her attorney said, "She's a disabled person." She was found mentally unfit to stand trial and escaped conviction.

Now she's missing.

All of this makes headlines because the media and the public decided to treat a mentally ill person as a mentally healthy person making "alternative choices." Instead of Teshu receiving the help she so obviously needed, the media chose to treat her as a unique flower blooming, and the public nodded along in order to appear tolerant—all the while laughing.

Teshu isn't alone.

In 2015, Sarah Boesveld of the National Post in Canada reported on a new phenomenon: "transabled" people, who feel that they've been born disabled people in healthy bodies. Some of these people cut off their own limbs. According to Boesveld: "Most crave an amputation or paralysis, though (one researcher) has interviewed one person wants his penis removed. Another wants to be blind. Many people ... arrange 'accidents' to help achieve the goal." According to the researcher, "this disorder is starting to be thought of as a neurological problem with the body's mapping, rather than a mental illness."

While Teshu and the transabled may seem fringe, transgenderism is quickly becoming mainstream. Media advocates for transgenderism as mental health say that men who believe they are women, for example, are actually women and ought to be treated as such, insisting that members of society refer to them using female pronouns. In December, the 6th U.S. Circuit Court of Appeals determined that an Ohio school district must let a young girl continue to use the restroom of her choice, stating that to prevent it would "further confuse a young girl with special needs ... and subject her to further irreparable harm." The young girl in question is a boy who believes she is a girl.

None of this is an argument for governmental intervention. It *is* an argument for society to stop treating mental illness as mental health—for the good of the mentally ill. Delusions should not be treated as reality. And treatments that do not work (transgender surgery has no impact on suicide rate, for example) should not be treated as solutions, particularly when those treatments are applied to children.

That does not mean that good solutions have been found for many of these mental illnesses. But to stop searching for good solutions and deem the problem solved by virtue of instilling the normalcy of the illness is counterproductive and dangerous.

My grandfather was hospitalized for paranoid schizophrenia in the 1960s. He thought he heard the radio talking to him. Today's society would presumably determine that a lifestyle choice and celebrate his diversity rather than getting him the lithium treatment he required, which saved his family. A society that thinks itself kind while treating mental illness as "letting your freak flag fly" and all the while silently snickering at the supposed freaks is a cruel society indeed.

Why the Image of the Great Economic Leader Is Dangerous

January 12, 2017

On Tuesday, Alibaba CEO Jack Ma, one of the richest men on the planet, met with President-elect Donald Trump at Trump Tower. After emerging from the meeting, he stood alongside Trump and announced: "We specifically talked about ... supporting 1 million small businesses, especially in the Midwest of America. Small businesses on the platform selling products—agriculture products and American services—to China and Asia because we're pretty big in Asia." Trump shook Ma's hand in front of the cameras and announced, "Jack and I are going to do some great things," before shaking hands.

This is good news, obviously. Bringing investment to the United States is worthwhile, and opening trade is excellent. The minipresser was skimpy on details, as most of Trump's economic big-win meetings have been. What does Ma get in return for the headline? Or is he simply moving toward investment in the United States on the basis of broad-based economic policy, including deregulation, from Trump?

There is one big problem with photo ops like this: They promote the myth that great men run the economy.

Since Trump's election, he has met at Trump Tower with CEOs from major companies and then trotted them out to the press, shaken their hands and announced new investments. This is in Trump's interest—he gets terrific headlines about how his very presence has boosted the economy. It's in the interest of the individual companies, too—they are on the good graces of the president-elect, plus they get the halo effect of being perceived as more patriotic and self-sacrificing.

But this routine creates the impression that the economy is essentially a series of negotiations between the president of the United States and individual companies, that the economy is, in simple terms, a rigged game. Advocates for such optics thrill to them. Isn't it showing that Trump is business-friendly? Doesn't it demonstrate that an activist commander in chief can bring the economy roaring back so long as he exerts the force of his will?

It's the force-of-will argument that's troubling to advocates of economic freedom. Economies do not thrive because command-and-control businessmen determine the fortunes of individual companies, or because they threaten individual businesses with governmental repercussions if they dare to engage in profit-maximizing activities. Economies thrive because of broad, consistent policies that create reward for positive risk-taking and increased productivity.

But the aesthetic of the Great Leader standing beside the Great Businessman runs precisely contrary to this reality. It fulfills a public thirst for someone to run things, even though that thirst generates an outsized picture of what the president can and should do. The aesthetic perpetuates an ugly cycle: Great Leader purportedly runs the economy in coordination with business; economy goes south; Great Leader blames business; public calls for more power for Great Leader; and businesses are called onto the carpet to make concessions to the Great Leader. All of this generates a less free, less dynamic economy.

We can all cheer news that more companies want to invest in the United States; we can all hope and pray that Donald Trump's economic policy draws more dollars and jobs to the country. But we should *not* fall prey to the economic misconception that the president ought to act as a benevolent economic dictator, bestowing favor upon all those who please him.

The Left Can't Help Overplaying its Hand

January 18, 2017

This week, Rep. John Lewis, D-Ga., accused President-elect Donald Trump of being an illegitimate president. He said: "I think the Russians participated in helping this man get elected. And they helped destroy the candidacy of Hillary Clinton. ... When you see something that is not right, not fair, not just, you have a moral obligation to do something."

Lewis wasn't the only person claiming that Trump had been elected illegitimately. New York Times columnist Paul Krugman, who just last week was preaching about why it's important to "(be) a mensch," wrote that it is "an act of patriotism" to "declare the man about to move into the White House illegitimate." Jehmu Greene, a Democratic National Committee chair candidate, said that Trump was "allegedly elected."

In response, another DNC chair candidate, Rep. Keith Ellison, D-Minn., upped the ante. He said he wouldn't be attending the inauguration because "(He) will not celebrate a man who preaches a politics of division and hate." Ellison spent most of his career lauding the hateful and divisive Nation of Islam.

Meanwhile, Trump met with Martin Luther King III at Trump Tower; King emerged in the lobby after the meeting and explained: "(Trump) said that he is going to represent all Americans. ... I believe that's his intent, but I think we also have to consistently engage with pressure, public pressure." Trump also met with entertainer Steve Harvey; they discussed poverty and incoming Housing and Urban Development Secretary Dr. Ben Carson, and Harvey then stated: "I found him in our meeting both congenial and sincere. Trump wants to help with the situations in the inner cities. ...

I walked away feeling like I had just talked with a man who genuinely wants to make a difference in this area."

So, do most Americans believe that Trump is a vicious racist, an illegitimate president who must be treated with scorn and disdain? Of course not. While Trump is highly unpopular for an incoming president—he has the lowest approval rating in modern history, at 40 percent—nearly all Americans think Trump was elected legitimately. A majority of them don't think Trump is racist.

Yet the left continues to double down on fiction instead of banking on fact.

In the past, the media and the Democrats were able to peddle extreme fictions because they had more powerful bullhorns than their targets. Former Gov. Mitt Romney could safely be labeled a tax cheat by Sen. Harry Reid, D-Nev., without fear of being blasted with a public relations tsunami; Vice President Joe Biden could state that Romney wanted to put black people back in chains; President Barack Obama could lie about the state of U.S.-Russia relations; the media could trot out old, unsubstantiated stories about Romney's supposed gay-bashing. And Romney couldn't do a thing.

That's not the case with Trump. Love him or hate him, Trump knows how to get attention, and his 20 million followers on Twitter give him quicker access to a wider audience than virtually any single media outlet or personality. That means the media and the Democrats need to button up their criticism rather than throw the kitchen sink.

But they're used to throwing the kitchen sink.

One problem: Trump has a public relations trebuchet, and he'll simply launch every kitchen appliance available in response.

If the left wants to keep marginalizing itself, it ought to continue leveling every radical allegation it can find against Trump. If the left wants to defeat Trump, it should stick to the facts.

Given recent history, that seems highly unlikely.

The Left's Vagina-Based Politics Demeans Women

January 25, 2017

Last Saturday, in an attempt to demonstrate outrage at ... at ... well, at *something*, some three million people across the country, mostly women, participated in women's marches. The scattershot platform for the march included public funding for contraception and abortion, equal pay, protections for illegal immigrants, anti-Israel activism and taxpayer-subsidized tampons, among other disparate causes. What united them? Hatred for the reality that Donald Trump was sworn in as president of the United States on Friday.

Two contrasting images emerged from the march itself: first, people filling the streets out of pure, unadulterated but vaguely motivated frustration; second, some of the most egregiously perverse speeches and signage in modern political history. While the left celebrated the first image—isn't this a sign of a political uprising in the making?—it ignored the second image, which is far more likely to backfire than to generate enthusiasm.

That second image was promulgated by celebrities like Ashley Judd, who was once considered a frontrunner for the Democratic nomination for the Senate in Kentucky. The has-been actress raged: "I am a nasty woman. ... I didn't know devils could be resurrected, but I feel Hitler in these streets. A mustache traded for a toupee. ... I am nasty like the bloodstains on my bed sheets. We don't actually choose if and when to have our periods. Believe me, if we could, some of us would. We do not like throwing away our favorite pairs of underpants. Tell me, why are pads and tampons still taxed when Viagra and Rogaine are not?"

Meanwhile, thousands of women donned "p——hats," or pink knit caps with cat ears, designed to rebuke Trump for the "Access Hollywood" tape in which he said he could grab women "by the p——" and get away with it. They marched with signs reading, "Leave My P—— Alone" and "If abortion is murder then b—-jobs are cannibalism" and "This P—— Bites And She Slays." NARAL Pro-Choice America handed out signs with similar messages.

This reduction of women to their constituent body parts is particularly ironic coming from the same side of the political aisle that declares that men sometimes have vaginas and that some women have penises. But more importantly, reducing female priorities to killing babies and increased funding for maxi pads merely objectifies women. Instead of recognizing that women have all sorts of political views, instead of recognizing that many women believe that they ought to be left alone by government in order to pursue their dreams, the women's marches declared that government has to treat vaginal possession with a sort of victim status, deserving of special protection.

The suggestion that the government must guarantee special privileges for women because their biology makes them somehow lesser, or that abortion rights are necessary to achieve equality, reduces the fight for female equality to the fight for female *sameness*. That's insulting to women.

And it's off-putting to voters. If these women are so concerned about vulgarity, why do they embrace it? If they're so upset that Trump supposedly reduces women to body parts, why promote that same silly thinking?

The left tried to run on the War on Women in 2016 and lost. Now they're doubling down. But apparently, so long as they can pat themselves on the back for their unearned moral superiority, they'll be happy.

The Left Won't Stop Threatening Violence Against Trump

February 1, 2017

We're barely a week and a half into President Trump's administration, and the left is in sheer panic mode. We've seen headlines blaring that Trump instituted a Muslim ban (he didn't). We've seen speculation that the Trump White House's failure to clearly inform the Department of Homeland Security how to implement his immigration executive order amounts to an attempted coup (nope). We've seen accusations that Trump will overthrow the judiciary, run roughshod over Congress and generally make a fascist nuisance of himself.

This isn't good for the country.

That's because if you think Trump is Literally Hitler, you're more likely to endorse violence against him and his allies, which is precisely what leftists have begun doing. At the Screen Actors Guild Awards, "Stranger Things" star David Harbour threatened Trump supporters over his immigration/refugee executive order, saying, "And when we are lost amidst the hypocrisy and the casual violence of certain individuals and institutions, we will, as per Chief Jim Hopper, punch some people in the face when they seek to destroy the meek and the disenfranchised and the marginalized." Madonna spoke at the Women's March on Washington, saying that she has "thought an awful lot about blowing up the White House." Robert De Niro said back in October that he'd like to "punch (Trump) in the face." Actress Lea DeLaria of "Orange Is the New Black" said that she wanted to "pick up a baseball bat and take out every f—king republican and independent I see."

Violence only becomes acceptable in the minds of most people if they are the victims. And not just victims—ultimate victims. They must have no other option. That means that playing up the threat of a Trumpocalypse means heightening the likelihood of violence. And we have indeed seen isolated incidents of anti-Trump violence around the country, dating all the way back to the campaign, when the media simply ignored Black Lives Matter movement attempts to shut down Trump campaign events.

Once we have reached the point where overt tearing of the social fabric is seen by half the country as morally decent, there is no more social fabric to tear. Civilization is actually on the ropes.

Which means that everybody has an obligation to calm the hell down.

Civilization isn't going to end because many Americans don't like Trump's policies. And Americans still have the ability to resist politically without engaging in violence. The left believes that it has a monopoly on nonofficial violence, which is why former President Barack Obama shied away from the harsh condemnation of riots in major American cities. But all that did was fray the social fabric to the point where tribalism has become mainstream political discourse.

Now we're even a step beyond that. No longer does the left restrict its vision of political violence to the already-immoral claim that downtrodden black folks in failing cities should be given "space to destroy." Upper-class elites at the SAG Awards have permission to engage in violent rhetoric. Everybody is capable of getting violent now that Trump is here.

Which means that political violence will likely increase. Which, counterproductively for the left, means that Trump will use the power at his disposal to restore law and order. And so the cycle will continue.

Can the Super Bowl Save America?

February 8, 2017

It's been several decades since American politics has been so contentious. According to a Reuters/Ipsos poll taken after President Trump's election, 32 percent of California residents want the state to secede from America. In the middle of the election cycle, Public Policy Polling found that 40 percent of Texans would have wanted the state to leave the country if Hillary Clinton had won—and that included 61 percent of Trump supporters. Nationally, 22 percent of people now want to see their particular state leave the union.

All of this is pervading our private lives. One post-election survey showed that nearly 1 in 3 Democrat women have cut someone out of their lives on social media over Trump's election. A September poll from the Monmouth University Polling Institute found that 70 percent of Americans think the election cycle has made America worse.

But we've been able to get together on some things.

We seemed to put aside political differences during the World Series, for example. That communal event—sitting around our televisions watching the greatest Game 7 in baseball history—seemed to unify us. The same thing happened this week with the Super Bowl. We all got together and watched Tom Brady give a performance for the ages, and for a short moment, we got along.

So, here's the question: Is that moment a chimera?

I've long been an antagonist of the notion that bouncing balls can somehow heal real political divisions. In 2007, I wrote this about the World Cup, saying: "Sports solve no great moral dilemmas. Sports are not politics."

That's still true.

But sports *can* provide a breath. Sometimes that breath is actually counterproductive—you wouldn't want a sporting event in 1944 between the United States and Germany to have delayed the liberation of the Nazi death camps by a week. But in America, that breath is highly necessary.

That's because the left has spent so long politicizing every element of American life that we're going to need some space, either physical or temporal. Americans seem willing to part from their neighbors because they believe their neighbors are in a heightened state of readiness to bother them. Texans think Californians want to control how they raise their children; Californians think Texans want to dirty their air. Federalism normally provides the distance for both sides to leave each other alone. But our common culture has shrunk that distance. Now you can't turn on the TV in Dallas without hearing a Los Angeles point of view.

The Super Bowl provided that distance. Thanks to President Trump's election, the Super Bowl organizers clearly recognized—for once—that they'd be best off eschewing politics rather than enabling Beyonce to dance around in Black Panther gear. Lady Gaga did an apolitical halftime show. The game was great. The politics were relegated to easily debunked commercials.

And we all took a breath.

Hollywood and pop culture would do well to remind themselves that if they don't want to alienate half their audience and exacerbate our differences, they can allow us room to breathe. The Super Bowl did that this year. For that, we should be just a little grateful, even if it didn't solve any true underlying problems. Those will require a bit more time and a bit more space.

How Presidents Shape
Their Administrations

February 15, 2017,

President Trump, we're told by his greatest advocates, will bring much-needed change. Why not merely ignore his rhetorical failings, his unsurpassed egotism, his confident ignorance? There's a good deal that's tempting about this proposal—who wouldn't want to separate the wheat from the chaff? I'm personally on board with perhaps three-quarters of Trump's policy implementation thus far in his presidency, even though I'm deeply concerned by his personal shortcomings. So why not just excise the shortcomings from the roll call?

There's one simple reason: Bureaucrats work toward their bosses. That's as true in the case of authoritarians as it is of democratically elected presidents. Those who live lower on the food chain of the executive branch know that their career advancement is dependent on pleasing the boss. This makes forecasting his desires key to self-preservation.

During President Obama's administration, his underlings attempted to do his bidding without waiting for explicit orders. That's why the IRS targeted conservative charities based on his general statements about Citizens United—they knew what Obama wanted, and they attempted to fulfill his wishes without a smoking gun order.

And indeed, that's what we see from those surrounding President Trump. Rather than hemming him in, they play to him, knowing that if they don't, they're likely to find themselves the recipients of an "Apprentice"-style firing.

Trump is absolutely conspicuous in encouraging such tactics. This week, for example, his senior adviser Kellyanne Conway appeared on national television to slam Nordstrom for its decision to drop Ivanka Trump's fashion line. Conway stated on "Fox & Friends": "Go buy Ivanka's stuff, is what I would tell you. I hate shopping, but I'm going to go get some for myself today. ... I'm going to give it a free commercial here. Go buy it today." After allegations that this violated federal law, the administration released a statement explaining that Conway had been "counseled." Trump then signaled that he was overweeningly happy with Conway.

The following Sunday, Trump's senior policy advisor, Stephen Miller, made the rounds on the news shows that Trump so conspicuously watches. There, he assured the audience in fully Trumpian language that Trump's power would brook no dissent. Glaring into camera with the confidence of Admiral Motti in "Star Wars" bragging about the Death Star, Miller explained, "I think to say that we're in control would be a substantial understatement." He then added, "our opponents, the media and the whole world will soon see as we begin to take further actions, that the powers of the president to protect our country are very substantial and will not be questioned." He bragged that we will once again have "unquestioned military strength beyond anything anybody can imagine." He said Trump has "accomplished more in just a few weeks than many presidents accomplish in an entire administration." This rather purple language made Trump feel just swell—he tweeted out his congratulations to Miller personally.

Then there was Sean Spicer, Trump's unlucky press secretary, who caved to Trump's ego in the first week and ripped into the media for supposedly underestimating the inauguration crowd size— a particularly sore spot for Trump, obviously. Spicer's awkwardly overheated appearance led Melissa McCarthy to target him on "Saturday Night Live," to the reported discomfort of the president.

All of this is to say that Trump's personality will shape this administration. And that's not a good thing for policy, since he values loyalty over policy and enthusiastic sycophancy over competence. We can only hope that we get some good policy out of Trump before his insecurities overwhelm his administration. Or we can pray that he finally lets those insecurities go and focuses on governing for the benefit of Americans, rather than assuaging his ego and encouraging others to do the same.

What If There's No Plan?

February 22, 2017

"Nobody panics when things go according to plan, even if the plan is horrifying!" the Joker says in "The Dark Knight." "Introduce a little anarchy. Upset the established order, and everything becomes chaos."

Welcome to the Trump administration.

The media seem befuddled as to how the Trump administration handles its business. Upset with the idea that Donald Trump is president, the press have sought a shadow "master planner" in the White House, and they've settled on White House chief strategist Steve Bannon. During the campaign, they suggested that the great mind was then-Trump campaign manager Kellyanne Conway. Sometimes, they say, it's White House senior policy advisor Stephen Miller.

Meanwhile, they see every Trumpian tweet and utterance as 4-D chess. When Trump tweets that the media are the enemy, the media immediately assume Trump has some sort of nefarious plan to quash the First Amendment. When a shoddy report breaks saying that Trump may make federal forces available to work alongside states in cracking down on illegal immigration, they rush to the notion that Trump has formed a deportation squad. When Trump's team rolls out a horribly flawed executive order on immigration from Muslim-majority countries, they immediately conclude that Trump is implementing a Muslim ban.

And what of Trump's bizarre, nonsensical tweets, the ones that don't introduce a new policy? Those are distractions, masterful attempts to hold a shiny object before the public while he plans evil deeds behind the curtain.

Then there are personnel issues. When Trump fires his national security advisor, Michael Flynn, the theories fly fast and furious. Flynn's connections to Russian President Vladimir Putin will expose Trump, so Trump had to throw him under the bus! Trump *had* to know something, didn't he?

Here's another theory: What if chaos is just chaos?

What if there's no master plan?

What if Trump is finding his way, one step at a time, along a path that 44 other men have traveled, some more slowly than others? What if Trump isn't an ideologue or a philosopher—and what if nobody around him is either? What if it's all just haphazard and chaotic, and what if we don't yet know what this administration will look like?

Is it possible that Trump is simply doing some good things and some bad things, and that he's saying silly things because that's what he does? Is it at all plausible that Trump is the president, not Steve Bannon or Kellyanne Conway or chief of staff Reince Priebus or anybody else, and that because Trump's an amateur at government he's unsure which way to step? Could it be that Trump isn't playing 4-D chess, that he's just a Wookie threatening to upend the board and rip his opponents' arms out of their sockets? He has been known to do that.

All of this is to say, let's all take a deep breath.

Here's the thing: Trump may not have a plan. He probably doesn't. Those around him probably have their own plans, but they're not the president. But you know who *did* have a plan? The people who constructed our constitutional system, placed checks and balances in that system and ensured that no one person could wield all power in American government. That means that even the presidency that begins most chaotically can find its sea legs, and even the presidencies that remain chaotic can't do too much damage.

So let's not panic. Everything's not chaos, even if it feels like it.

Trump Is Winning,
and Leftists Are Confused

March 1, 2017

President Trump's approval ratings are nothing special. Actually, they're extraordinarily low by historical standards—he's clocking in at 44 percent, according to the latest NBC News/Wall Street Journal poll. His support base is highly polarized, with 85 percent of Republicans behind him and just 9 percent of Democrats. If those rates drop steadily for the next two years—and given the level of polarization, they certainly could—Republicans would be in serious danger of losing the House, since low presidential approval ratings correlate significantly with House elections.

Then again, Trump's support base may be stable.

Here's why.

According to that same poll, approximately 57 percent of voters say that Trump is doing about as well as they expected. Meanwhile, his approval ratings far outclass those of Congress, which has just a 29 percent approval rating. That's a nonpartisan statistic. And thirty-one percent approve of Democrats in Congress, while 32 percent approve of Republicans in Congress. The most unpopular figure in American politics remains House Minority Leader Nancy Pelosi, D-Calif., with 19 percent who feel positively about her in any way against 44 percent who feel negatively about her. The Democratic Party's negatives double up the Republican Party's.

This relatively positive feeling toward Republicans means that 60 percent of respondents are hopeful and optimistic about the future of the country, and 40 percent are pessimistic. And that's with a sample that shows just 37 percent of respondents who voted for Trump in the presidential election.

None of this says that everybody is comfortable with Trump. Fifty-two percent say that Trump's chaotic style is "unique to this administration and (suggests) real problems." But the American people largely agree with Trump's agenda. Eighty-six percent say that "a small group in our nation's capital has reaped the rewards of government while the people have borne the cost." Fifty-three percent say that "the news media and other elites are exaggerating the problems with the Trump Administration because they are uncomfortable and threatened with the kind of change that Trump represents." While 37 percent of respondents say that they want Democrats in Congress setting the agenda, 19 percent say that Republicans in Congress should do so, and 37 percent say that Trump should do so. Fifty-seven percent of Americans say Trump is likely to bring change—and 63 percent of those people say he will bring the right kind of change. Forty-one percent of Americans say the economy will get better, and 73 percent of those attribute that prospective success to Trump. Only 4 percent of Americans think Obamacare works well the way it is. And here's the best statistic of all for Trump personally: Thirty-eight percent of Americans say they like him personally regardless of whether they like or dislike his policies.

All of this suggests that Americans are giving Trump a chance, and that they're tired of the media failing to do so. They think Trump is going to bring change, and they want to allow him freedom to pursue that change. Democrats and members of the media who keep saying that Trump can't be trusted with the tiller of government ought to have an easy solution: Give him all the leeway he wants, and then watch him pursue policies they think are unpopular. By acting as foils for Trump, the media and the left actually prop him up—they allow him to position them as obstacles to making change.

Trump is in control. The American people are ready to see him perform. Now it's time for him to step up and create the change he's preached for so long.

The 5 Stages of a Trump Scandal

March 8, 2017

Another week, another "nothing burger" Trump scandal.

This week, President Trump took to Twitter to accuse former President Obama of ordering him to be wiretapped at Trump Tower. That accusation, of course, had no evidence to support it. But instead of merely stating that the accusation was false, the media responded with volcanic rage, declaring that it was *outrageous* to suggest that Obama would *ever* have done such a thing. To this, conservatives rightly responded saying that Obama has a long history of targeting enemies through bureaucratic surrogates, and that multiple media reports stated that the Obama Department of Justice sought FISA warrants against Trump associates. To this, leftists responded by accusing conservatives of covering for Trump's lies.

And so it goes.

This is the typical Trump scandal. It has five stages:

Stage one: A media outlet of Trump's liking reports something.

Stage two: Trump simplifies that report into an incorrect headline.

Stage three: The media jump on the incorrect headline, tacitly suggesting that there is *no* relationship between Trump's headline and the truth.

Stage four: The right fires by pointing out that while Trump may be getting the headline wrong, there's underlying truth to the narrative.

Stage five: The left seethes that anyone would defend Trump's falsehoods.

And then we repeat this routine over and over, further ensconcing ourselves in our partisan bubbles.

We saw this exact pattern just two weeks ago, when Trump saw a piece on Fox News' "Tucker Carlson Tonight" during which video journalist Ami Horowitz traveled to Sweden and talked about rising crime rates related to increased Muslim immigration. Trump took that in, processed it and then blurted out that something awful had happened "last night in Sweden." The media quickly declared that not only had nothing bad happened in Sweden the prior night but that there was also *no* evidence of a serious crime problem in Sweden due to Muslim immigration. To this, the right responded with statistics showing that Sweden did indeed have a rising crime problem, and that lack of statistics did not denote lack of crime but rather politically driven lack of reporting. The media then asked incredulously whether the right would continue to defend Trump's nonsense.

Now, note that nothing here is actually scandalous. Trump will always play fast and loose with the truth; the media will always split hairs in order to declare Trump's entire program out of bounds; and the right will generally defend Trump's larger program. But it does point out a lack of truth telling on all sides because at any stage of this process, the scandal could die. Trump could simply speak accurately. The left could point out Trump's inaccuracies while telling the whole story. The right could do the same.

But because Trump has become such a controversial litmus test, everyone's reacting to Trump rather than to the truth. That means truth becomes secondary, which actually *helps* Trump, since his commitment to the truth is less than strict.

It's time to get beyond this cycle of stupidity. Next time Trump tweets something silly, everybody ought to simply take a deep breath—both left and right. Instead of letting Trump's Twitter feed choose the battleground over facts, Americans on both sides ought to decipher facts and then fight over narrative. That's what decent politics would look like.

Are We on the Verge of Violence?

March 15, 2017

Two weeks ago, political scientist Charles Murray of the American Enterprise Institute went to speak at Middlebury College. There, he was quickly surrounded by protesters chanting: "Racist, sexist, anti-gay. Charles Murray, go away!" On his way out of the venue, a violent throng surrounded him and his security, as well as one of the university professors. She ended up in a neck brace. The same week, supporters of President Trump held a rally in Berkeley, California, and anti-Trump protesters threw smoke bombs and began punching people.

This sort of political violence is becoming more and more common around the country. I've personally been smuggled onto and off the California State University, Los Angeles campus during a near-riot caused by one of my speeches. When a fellow guest on CNN's HLN grabbed me by the back of the neck on national television in 2015, leftist commentators celebrated. In Berkeley, we saw Antifa rioters run roughshod through the town in honor of an upcoming visit by provocateur Milo Yiannopoulos. During the presidential campaign, we saw a Trump event in Chicago shut down by leftists who were intent on causing havoc, and we saw Trump supporters beaten in the streets in San Jose. Meanwhile, we saw Trump himself encouraging supporters to punch protesters and vowing to defend those who followed through from legal charges.

When despicable white supremacist Richard Spencer was punched on a city street in Washington D.C., the media quickly began asking whether it was OK to punch a Nazi. And many Americans concluded that it was fine. After all, Captain America did it!

Here's the problem: Once we start punching one another, there are only two ways such violence ends. First, an overarching powerful government could step in to stop the violence, to the cheers of the group represented by it. Second, one of the sides could literally club the other into submission. Both solutions are anti-American and frightening.

Not all ideas are created equal. Some are terrible and should be dismissed. But that's not the same thing as *banning* ideas or treating them with violence. In fact, the irony of those who claim to be doing political violence in the name of freedom is that political violence between citizens never ends in freedom—it nearly always ends in tyranny.

The rise of the Nazis was preceded by heavy violence in Weimar Germany between communist bands and brownshirts. The two sides would go to each others' rallies and speeches and launch into serious bloodbaths in which people were killed. Brownshirts deliberately started violence with communists in order to draw supporters to their cause. They used that violence to create martyrs (Horst Wessel was the most famous) and prey on the reality of communist violence to seize power.

America isn't Weimar. Law and order still prevails. But if we want America to remain a free country, we're going to have to back away from violence, condemn it roundly on all sides and kill the notion that ideas must be fought with fists rather than other ideas.

Why Does It Feel Like Everything's a Scandal?

March 22, 2017

Over the past two weeks, Democrats have begun to acknowledge that they have virtually no evidence demonstrating meaningful collusion between the Trump campaign and the Russian government. They proclaim that circumstantial evidence shows ties between Trump staffers and President Vladimir Putin—former Trump campaign manager Paul Manafort and former Trump advisor Roger Stone allegedly had significant contacts with the Russians. But to this point, they've got nothing.

Meanwhile, the FBI director and head of the National Security Agency announced that they had no evidence that Trump Tower was wiretapped by former President Obama. Mike Rogers, the NSA head, agreed that any accusations of British intelligence involvement in Trump wiretapping is "ridiculous." Republicans point to the fact that there were multiple media reports of Trump associates being caught on wiretap. But to this point, they've got nothing.

Scandals that catch fire require two elements: first, confirmation of a widely held suspicion about a politician's character; second, actual evidence of nefarious behavior. Hillary Clinton's email scandal damaged her significantly because of her long record of untrustworthy behavior, including destruction of records. Bill Clinton's sex scandal damaged him because he had a long history of lying about his sexual conduct.

Other scandals simply never gained steam because they lacked the requisite plausibility, even if the evidence was sufficient. Yes, the IRS should have damaged President Obama. But the central contention that Obama used government as an instrument to target his opposition never took hold of the public imagination. Sure, Iran-Contra should have severely tarnished President Reagan. But Americans didn't buy the notion of Reagan as a great international manipulator. In short, politicians we trust more are less likely to suffer from severe scandal.

And herein lies the problem: In an era in which half of the population will believe virtually everything about the other side, we're primed for scandal *all the time*. The tinder of scandal is dry, and everyone is just waiting nervously for a lit match to set the blaze. That means a whiff of scandal pervades nearly everything. Otherwise-innocuous behavior seems laden with sinful potential. And those who claim wrongdoing about those on the other side gain additional credibility *no matter the evidence of what they claim*.

That means the conspiracy theorists gain ground while honesty loses. Those on the left willing to accuse President Trump of Kremlin connections sans evidence earn the love and support of those on their own side of the aisle; and those on the right willing to humor Trump's most extreme claims about Obama's wiretapping gain clicks and admiration on their side. The result: Those who suggest that we wait for evidence are seen as gullible, naive.

In this context, the space for rational conversation shrinks down to a thimble. Instead of the left dismissing President Trump's stupidities as stupidities, Trump becomes a nefarious character seeking doom; instead of the right acknowledging that intelligence could have swept up some Trump contacts in its pursuit of Russian interference, the entire intelligence community becomes a big blob of statist corruption. No mistake is honest; every action must be interpreted in the darkest possible way.

If this leads to an American return to smaller government—hey, we can't trust anybody anyway, so let's stop handing them power—this new paranoia might be acceptable. But it won't. Instead, Americans seems bound and determined to hand power to those on each side who are most apt to identify the nefarious intentions of those on the other side, with or without evidence. That's a recipe for not only polarization but also political breakdown.

When Does Trump Become the Establishment?

March 29, 2017

Let's pretend.

It's January 2017, and President Jeb Bush just took office.

After conceding to his right flank during the election cycle that he would move to overturn President Obama's Deferred Action for Childhood Arrivals program, Bush immediately backtracks and does nothing. Attempting to fulfill a campaign promise, he then pushes a bill that would supposedly repeal and replace Obamacare, except that the bill does no such thing. Instead, it makes significant changes to Medicaid but re-enshrines the central provisions of Obamacare while also creating a new entitlement program. The bill earns the support of establishment stalwarts ranging from House Speaker Paul Ryan, R-Wis., to Senate Majority Leader Mitch McConnell, R-Ky.

Conservatives revolt. They tell Bush that they won't stand by for Obamacare 2.0—they promised repeal and replace, and they'll fulfill their promise. And Bush responds by issuing an ultimatum: It's either this bill or nothing. He'll let Obamacare stand.

Who thinks talk radio would be split? Who believes that Fox News' top hosts would spend the evening stumping for the bill? Who thinks that Bush would be blamed rather than Ryan or McConnell?

If the House Freedom Caucus had defeated the bill, who thinks that many of the anti-establishment conservatives would have mourned?

And if Bush and his top surrogates had then spent the weekend talking about dumping the Freedom Caucus to work with Democrats, who thinks conservatives would have resignedly nodded along?

Of course they wouldn't have. They would have rightly labeled Bush an avatar of the establishment. They would have criticized him for selling out his base, abandoning his supporters and playing to the cocktail party circuit. They would have ripped him up.

But Bush isn't president. Donald Trump is. And because Trump played an anti-establishment figure on TV, too many conservatives assume he is one.

He isn't. President Trump is anti-establishment when it comes to persona, of course—he thinks that every governmental Gordian knot can be cut, that he can simply bulldoze his opposition, that deals are for sissies and that tough guys finish first. But the deals he wants to cut look a lot more like former President George W. Bush's compassionate conservatism than they do like the tea party agenda.

And yet, many Americans keep treating Trump like an outsider. He isn't. He's the most powerful man on Earth, the head of the executive branch. He can't just keep yelling at Ryan and McConnell publicly while dealing with them on legislation that Jeb Bush would endorse in a heartbeat, and then rip conservatives who disagree. That doesn't make him anti-establishment. It just makes him a blowhard.

If Trump wants to represent the outsider, it's about time for him to represent those *outside of government.* And that means minimizing government power, not maximizing it. But that's the dirty little secret: Trump isn't anti-establishment; he's pro-establishment so long as he's the establishment.

On Human Nature and Mike Pence's Dinner Partners

April 5, 2017

This week, the Washington Post published a long form piece about Vice President Mike Pence, which included a little tidbit that said, "In 2002, Mike Pence told the Hill that he never eats alone with a woman other than his wife and that he won't attend events featuring alcohol without her by his side, either." The left—and some elements of the secular-minded right—lost its ever-loving mind. Bret Stephens of the Wall Street Journal said this "religious fundamentalism" springs from "terror of women." Joanna Grossman of Vox called Pence's rule "probably illegal," saying it is "deeply damaging to women's employment opportunities."

Never mind that there's no evidence whatsoever of employment discrimination by Pence against women. Never mind that Pence's 30-plus year marriage is good evidence that his standards have worked for him and his wife in preserving their marriage. Pence is bad, and his standards are bad. What's more, they're theocratic insanity that wouldn't be out of place in countries ruled by Shariah.

What absolute horse pucky.

Pence isn't saying that every dinner with a woman potentially ends in the boudoir. He's saying that human beings are fallible, that they become particularly fallible away from their spouses in the wee hours, and that they become even more fallible than that around alcohol.

But this is one of the great foolish myths propagated by the left and now humored by even some on the right: that risk assessment by individual human beings, examining their own hearts, amounts to discrimination; that those who want to guard themselves from situations in which they are more likely to sin are somehow propagating societal myths.

It isn't true. Human beings sin. They sin because they are tempted. And they are tempted because they refuse to perform an honest assessment of their own hearts. Not all personal situations are created equal. A late-night dinner involving alcohol with a work colleague of the sex to which you could be attracted obviously carries more risk than working in the office with that same person in the middle of the day. Even leftists understand this, which is why there are significant restrictions on campus regarding male professors alone with female students and student-professor dating. As Damon Linker of The Week states: "What if morality requires social and cultural supports that limit individual freedom and that secular liberals are unwilling to forgo? ... Perhaps Pence's more morally traditional outlook has something in its favor—namely, realism."

Yet the left denies realism. It says that if Pence is tempted, that merely shows that his marriage is weak. The left's own logic with regard to sexual urges states that such urges are undeniable—so Pence must be perfect and asexual outside of marriage, or marriage itself is restrictive and nasty. To prove that his marriage is solid, therefore, Pence should be able to walk through a strip club without ever feeling a shred of temptation.

This is asinine. It's not how marriage works, and it's not how human beings work. It's not how life works, either. The left casts all individual sins at the feet of society, so it thinks that any prospective adultery must be the result of monogamy's evils or society's sexism. But no matter how you change social mores, people will sin and those they love will be hurt.

Unless, that is, people recognize their own limitations and set fences around themselves. That's not an act of discrimination or evil. That's an act of love—for a spouse, for a society and for a culture of decency that requires that we all take a long, hard look in the mirror before determining that we are incapable of sin.

The Insanity of the Left's Child Gender-Confusion Agenda

April 12, 2017

On Sunday, The New York Times ran a piece by Jack Turban, a research fellow at the Yale School of Medicine. Turban says that doctors should begin applying puberty blockers to children who identify as transgender as early as possible. That's because, according to him, "it has become clear that if we support these children in their transgender identities instead of trying to change them, they thrive instead of struggling with anxiety and depression."

Turban uses as his example one 14-year-old girl named Hannah who was born a boy named Jonah. Turban glows: "Hannah is using a puberty-blocking implant and getting ready to embark on the path of developing a female body by starting estrogen. Ten years ago most doctors would have called this malpractice. New data has now made it the protocol for thousands of American children."

Ten years ago, doctors weren't embracing politically correct insanity as medicine.

Turban, you see, claims that by transforming children's bodies younger, we will help them avoid societal stigma, and that it's that stigma that's responsible for the shockingly high rates of suicide and depression associated with gender dysphoria. But there's no hard data to support that notion. A study from professors at the American Foundation for Suicide Prevention and the Williams Institute at the UCLA School of Law, for example, found that 46 percent of transgender men and 42 percent of transgender women in the study had attempted suicide.

Is this due to discrimination? The study does show high levels of discrimination against transgender people. But it *also* shows that the suicide rate among transgender women who say people identify them as transgender regularly is 45 percent. How about those who are able to pass for the gender to which they claim membership? Their suicide rate is *still 40 percent*. How about the suicide rate among those transgender individuals who have had hormone treatment? It's 45 percent. Surgery doesn't militate against suicide either.

But Turban has an agenda. And so, he cites one study of 63 transgender children, which found that if they were allowed to "socially transition"—if people treated them as their preferred sex— then they had indistinguishable levels of anxiety and depression from that of their peers. But this study concerns children, who have not yet experienced the rigors of sex drive and sexual dynamics; it also ignores the small sample size and the fact that a reported 8 in 10 children who experience gender confusion grow out of it. But Turban's fine with maintaining gender confusion for those 8 children out of 10 in order to preserve Hannah's peace of mind—even if Hannah might have grown out of her symptoms herself, thereby lowering risk of suicide over time.

This is science with an agenda.

Adults should be free to make decisions about their sexuality and their bodies. But children should not be subjected to the whims of politically driven adults when it comes to massive bodily mutilation that impairs function for a lifetime—all before the child has experienced puberty. And society should not be obligated to obey the gender theory nonsense of the radical left, which seeks to confuse as many children as possible in the name of an anti-biological program in service to a political agenda.

The Democrats Lose Their S—-

April 19, 2017

Donald Trump won the presidency because he was seen as blunt and non-manipulative, as opposed to the robotic, incompetent Machiavellianism of Hillary Clinton—and because he demonstrated that he cared about the concerns of Americans who were sick of being called racist sexist bigot homophobes for not paying obeisance to the leftist cause du jour.

Democrats apparently think he won because he said the word "s—-."

On Wednesday, the Democratic Party got into a Twitter war with the Republican Party. The GOP tweeted out a picture of a shirt sold by the Dem rats that says "Democrats give a sh*t about people." This is a takeoff on Democratic National Committee Chairman Tom Perez's statements that Republicans don't give a s—- about people. Republicans responded to the shirt by tweeting: "2016: 'When they go low, we go high'—Michelle Obama." The Democratic Party responded, "Taking away health care from 24 million people is going low. Giving a s—- about people is going high."

The theory here seems to be that repeating the same Democratic message but with a higher pitch and more vulgar language will win them political favor again. It wasn't Trump's rejection of leftism that won him acolytes; it was that he dropped the S-word and the F-word and the P-word. If only Democrats could imitate his style—all would be well!

This is asinine.

Cursing didn't hurt Trump because Trump was running *against* type. His cursing demonstrated that he wasn't a conservative fuddy-duddy who was deeply concerned about policing language. He channeled the anger of his base.

Democratic cursing just demonstrates, as always, that Democrats have no standards with regard to speech. It's not violating a taboo to say s——- as a Democrat because there is no taboo. And simply saying that word over and over doesn't help Democrats who are still struggling for a national message.

Democrats are in trouble nationwide because they have strayed from their core pitch: caring about every American. Instead, they have decided to embrace the intersectional nonsense of Barack Obama, who divvied Americans up along race, class, sex and sexual orientation lines and then pandered to each group individually. That program is both anti-American and insincere because to pander to each group means to shortchange them all. After all, what happens when Democrats claim that black Americans are victims of white society but that gay Americans are victims of straight society? Are black straight people the victims or the victimizers? Is the unemployed blue-collar white fellow who used to work a steel job in Indiana the victim because he's living on the edge of poverty, or is he the victimizer because he refuses to agree that a biological man can be a woman?

The Democrats no longer have a national message that resonates. They have regional messages that make most Americans feel like refuse. But because Democrats think that they'll only win by upping their "cool factor," they'll continue trotting out Sarah Silverman to make vagina jokes in a little girl voice while mocking Donald Trump and then believe they've won the cultural battle. They'll deploy Tom Perez to use other four-letter words.

And they'll keep losing.

Are We Really Living in Trump's America?

April 26, 2017

For the past few months, whenever someone on the left says something particularly insane, conservatives immediately snark back, "This is why Trump won." To a certain extent, they're right: The palpable anger on the radicalized left that helped govern America into political polarization drove the Trump movement. Trump sits in the White House as a result.

But there's a more important question that must be asked as we approach day 100 of the Trump administration: Has Trump actually changed anything in America?

The 100-day mark means little in reality. As Trump points out, it's an arbitrary deadline; there have been presidents who did little in their first 100 days and ended up with a solid legacy (Bill Clinton) and those who did an enormous amount and ended up imploding (Lyndon B. Johnson). But here's what the first 100 days *actually* do: They set the table.

President Ronald Reagan set the table for his administration by pushing for lower taxes over the protestations of the Democrats and militantly standing against Soviet aggression. President Clinton's failures in his first 100 days set the stage for his move to the center—by his second term, he declared that the "era of big government is over."

President Barack Obama came into office promising change. That change did not come chiefly in the realm of policy—his only lasting policy change appears to be Obamacare, which is currently bankrupting itself across the country—but in the political heart of the country. Before 2009, Americans yearned for unity. It's why Obama was elected. We were tired of the polarization of the Bush years; we were sick of the feeling that half the country wanted the other half gone. Obama pledged to change that.

That pledge came on the back of big-government promises. America could be united, Obama seemed to suggest, if only we believed in him personally. *That's* what Obama achieved in his first 100 days: He changed the nature of the political debate by suggesting that big government could earn your trust, that he would demonstrate the dedication necessary to turn government into an avatar of this newfound "unity."

Then he utilized government power to push for hardcore leftism, which polarized the country.

Obama's 100-day vision failed. But Trump has yet to replace it with anything new. Trump's "Make America Great Again" sloganeering hasn't promised a new unity of purpose. It has actually exacerbated a reverse polarization. His policies aren't discussed in terms of helping all Americans; they embody a political sectarianism pioneered by Obama and hijacked by Trump. Trump's first 100 days haven't moved the American story in any marked way at all, actually—we're precisely where we were 101 days ago. That doesn't mean he hasn't had policy victories (most obvious is the confirmation of Supreme Court Justice Neil Gorsuch). But it *does* mean that there is no vision upon which he calls Americans to the table. There are just things he wants and things he doesn't, and Americans he likes and Americans he doesn't.

If past trends hold, that means his administration will continue to be a haphazard agglomeration of random partisan prescriptions without any basis in a thoroughgoing vision of Americanism. We're all here, and he's the president, and that's that. But while such lack of vision can work in an oppositional setting, as a rejection of the status quo, it can't move America forward in any real way.

That's why Trump must decide what he wants America to be, not just what he wants Americans to think of him. He must provide a vision. If he doesn't, he'll be seen as merely a placeholder, a reactionary president living in an America of Barack Obama's making.

The Smug Blind Left Is Trump's Best Friend

May 3, 2017

On Saturday night, Samantha Bee hosted the much-ballyhooed "Not The White House Correspondents' Dinner." The dinner was retitled, of course, because President Trump wasn't enough of a rube to subject himself to three hours of barbs and put-downs by leftists who didn't vote for him and see him as a joke and disdain his voters.

At the dinner, Bee trotted out in a white pantsuit, looking like Kristin Chenoweth playing Hillary Clinton in an alternate-reality version of the 2016 election. "Your job has never been harder," she gushed to the assembled members of the self-pleasuring press. "You expose injustice against the weak, and you continue to fact-check the president as if he might someday get embarrassed. Tonight is for you."

Shortly after this ode to the bravery of journalists who maintained silence for eight years of President Barack Obama's lies on Iran and health care, and his Department of Justice targeting the Associated Press and Fox News, Bee appeared on CNN with Jake Tapper. There, she explained of her nearly unwatchable mess of a show, "Full Frontal": "I do the show for me and for people like me, and I don't care how the rest of the world sees it, quite frankly. ... We birth it, and then the world receives it however they want to receive it." During the entirety of this statement, a smug grin was plastered across her face.

Here's a basic rule of thumb: In order to be smug, you generally have to be unaware of your smugness. Bee fits the bill. So do the members of the White House press corps. There is plenty to question about President Trump's administration, from his shifting promises to his knee-jerk reversals, from his policy vagaries to his staffing chaos. But instead of approaching the American people as potential friends to be convinced, smug leftists treat them as ignoramuses. There's no sincerity involved. Every critique of Trump supporters lumps them all together, and then treats them as gum stuck to the bottom of the shoe of the republic.

Samantha Bee and company have the unmistakable air of the bullies from every high school and college comedy: preening self-obsessed rich kids who sneer at the "losers" who inhabit the hallways, and plan pool parties and taunt the poor kids who can't afford anything better than a beat-up Pinto. The journalist/Hollywood clique is Greg Marmalard from "Animal House," Rod from "Breaking Away" and Regina George from "Mean Girls." They're smug. They're liberal. And that's what drives Trump support.

Trump knows this. That's why he skipped the correspondents dinner and instead went to Pennsylvania, where he held a rally and hilariously declared, "A large group of Hollywood actors and Washington media are consoling each other in a hotel ballroom in our nation's capital right now." It was the best moment for Trump since his speech to a joint session of Congress.

Trump may not be popular among the cool kids. But he's cool enough among them to win supporters in the swing states. If the cool kids don't cut it out, they'll get eight years to mock him and be smug in their assurance that they know what the American people want better than they do.

Racism Is Only Racism If Comes From Groups the Left Hates

May 10, 2017

This week, an odd tweet appeared in my mentions from verified Twitter users—users prominent enough to be granted a blue check mark by Twitter itself. This one came courtesy of a rapper named Talib Kweli Greene. I'll admit I'd never heard of Greene until he suddenly appeared in my mentions calling me a "racist ass." It turns out Greene is a rapper with well over 1 million Twitter followers and a long history of "social activism."

A quick search of Greene's Twitter feed showed a wide variety of instances of the rapper calling people "white boy" and "coon." He says that this does not make him racist, of course—only the term "black boy" would be racist, since Greene maintains that white people cannot truly be victimized by racism. When I pointed out that seeming incongruity, Greene replied: "What's the problem white boy? You think 'white boy' is racist? Wow. You're dumber than I thought." He then dared me to call him "black boy," which, of course, I would never do, since that would be racist.

What's Greene's actual argument? It seems to be that since the derogatory slur "black boy" was thrown around by lynch mobs, any other derogatory slur can no longer be derogatory. This is the rhetorical equivalent of the argument your mother used to make back in grade school: You're not truly hungry, since there are children in China who are starving to death. The argument fails for the same reason: Yes, it turns out there are gradations of racism, just as there are gradations of hunger. But you *were* hungry when you were a kid, even if your bowels weren't distended, and you're a racist if you call someone "white boy" in a derogatory fashion, even if you're not attempting to lynch him.

Thanks to the theory of intersectionality, however, such logic goes by the wayside. Intersectional theory has now taken over the college campuses, leaving the broken corpses of decency and reason in its wake. Intersectionality classifies social categories of race, class, gender and sexual orientation into a hierarchy of victimhood that decides how you should be treated. If you are a black lesbian, for example, you outrank a black straight man and your view must be treated with more care and weight than that of the black straight man. More importantly, since society somehow classifies you as "lesser" than the black straight man, you are incapable of ever doing anything to victimize that black straight man—social powerlessness means that your individual victim status never changes.

This is why Greene and others on the left believe it's just fine to use "white boy" as a slur: Black people have historically seen discrimination in America that whites have not; whites benefit from a more powerful status in society at large; and therefore, black people cannot possibly be racist against white people. As Morehouse College Professor Dr. Marc Lamont-Hill said last year, "black people don't have the institutional power to be racist or to deploy racism."

There's only one problem with this notion: It's racist.

Racism bolstered by power is obviously more dangerous than racism without it. But racism can be used to achieve power, too— generally through the polarization of racial groups against one another. Tribalism is a powerful force, and resorting to a victimhood mentality to explain tribalism away doesn't make it any less toxic. The faster Americans learn that, the faster racism can actually be curbed rather than exacerbated.

Happy Legal Guardian of Unspecified Gender Day!

May 17, 2017

Mother's Day marks an awkward time of year for those on the hard left.

First, there are those who deny the value of motherhood. Cecile Richards of Planned Parenthood tweeted, "Nothing says 'I love you, Mom!' like standing up for the right of mothers everywhere to get the care they need." By this, presumably, she meant abortion care—Planned Parenthood performs hundreds of thousands of abortions every year. But there is one thing that says "I love you, Mom!" more than providing abortion care: babies who aren't aborted. It turns out that in order for the appellation mother to have any meaning, children must be part of the process.

Then there are those who believe that childbearing and child rearing aren't central to the female mission, that checking accounts receivable is more socially and individually rewarding. In this category we could put Ivanka Trump, who tweeted about the "wage gap" on Mother's Day, even though the only true reason for the difference in overall earnings between men and women is attributable to motherhood. It turns out that it may be worth families forgoing mom doing extra work at the office if she can spend more time at home with the kids. There's nothing wrong with that. In fact, it's worth celebrating.

But the fun—or lack thereof—doesn't stop there for the radical left. We still haven't dealt with the cisgender nature of Mother's Day. How could we suggest that women have anything special to celebrate when men can be women? After all, Dove has run an ad with a transgender woman explaining what motherhood means to her. A columnist for the Toronto Star, Emma Teitel, wrote this week that Mother's Day should be ditched in favor of Guardian's Day, since "gendered holidays" are "painful" and "exclusionary" and a "drag for non-binary parents who don't identify with a single gender." Teitel says, "A guardian can be a mom, a dad, a non-binary parent, a grandparent, an aunt, an uncle, a pet owner, or why the heck not—somebody who takes really good care of his houseplants."

But we're still not done. How about gay couples? What about children with two daddies? One Canadian school has reportedly ditched Mother's Day and Father's Day activities because they are not sufficiently inclusive. The administration announced via letter, "In an effort to celebrate diversity, inclusivity and also nurture our students who are part of non-traditional families, we have decided to encourage those celebrations to take place at home."

So, we've already done away with apple pie—far too much sugar for those growing children—and now we're doing away with motherhood. Do we have any values in common anymore?

Fortunately, most Americans reject this stupidity. Mothers are still mothers, and motherhood still has inherent and beautiful value. My wife is a doctor, which means she does the most important work there is, but she believes that her most important role is as a mother to our two children. She's right. It's amazing that our society has become so jaded about the value of motherhood that we're willing to overthrow it in favor of gender and sexual sensitivity, as well as increasing women's hours in the workplace.

No, You're Not a Bigot If You Only Want to Have Sex With People to Which You Are Attracted

May 24, 2017

You. Yes, you. You're a bigot.

Are you a straight man who only wants to have sex with women? Are you a gay man who only wants to have sex with men? Are you a bisexual man who wants to have sex with people of both sexes but only if they are good-looking? Are you asexual?

You're a bigot.

According to Samantha Allen of The Daily Beast, it is deeply "disappointing but unsurprising" that under 20 percent of Americans in a recent survey said they would be open to having sex with a transgender person. That's because, she says, "Cultural acceptance has tended to lag behind formal recognition."

It turns out that according to the left, all sexual behavior is malleable and based largely on social structures that have been implemented by the patriarchy. Men and women don't exist but for their self-perception—we know that a man can be a woman and a woman can be a man, regardless of biology. That's why Caitlyn Jenner isn't just a man with a mental disorder and some plastic surgery and hormone injections; Caitlyn Jenner is as much of a woman as Michelle Obama. The left reasons that if a man can be a woman, then a man who only wants to have sex with biological women must be a bigot—his desires have been wrongly defined by a society that restricted the definition of womanhood to, you know, women. If only men had been exposed to the deeper truth of gender earlier. If only they'd known that some women have male genitalia.

Then, perhaps they'd be willing to have sex with biological men who are actually women.

The same holds true with regard to homosexuals, of course. If a woman is a lesbian, it's discriminatory of her to not want to have sex with a man who identifies as a woman. Her desires have also been shaped by her environment. And her environment has drawn a stark but wrong—oh, ever so wrong!—line between biological men and biological women.

If all of this sounds insane, that's because it is. Straight men are attracted to women, not men who identify as women. Straight women are attracted to biological men. As a general rule, homosexuals are attracted to members of the same biological sex. Attempting to pretend away reality doesn't change that reality.

But the left is plagued by two myths that lie in direct opposition to one another. The first: All human behavior can be changed by changing society at large. The second: All human sexual behavior is innate and unchanging. Under the first myth, if we just train people that men and women are the same and that even their genitals don't provide a meaningful difference, men will begin having sex with transgender women, and women will begin having sex with transgender men. Under the second myth, however, transgender identity itself is immutable and unchanging, as is homosexuality and heterosexuality. This provides an unanswerable conundrum for transgender advocates: How can they get people to accept transgender people sexually when people's sexuality is supposedly unchanging?

So the left merely ignores the problem and papers it over with the word "bigot."

Reality isn't bigotry. People are attracted to those they are attracted to. There is a biological component to that as well as a cultural component. But ignoring biology in favor of culture is idiotic, and ignoring culture in favor of biology is ignorant. They both play a part. The suggestion that discriminatory nastiness is at the root of the perfectly logical biological desire for people to have sex with members of the opposite biological sex is merely a slur, a crutch to cover up the illogic of the far left when it comes to gender and sex.

How America Lost Its Head

May 31, 2017

In 2013, the left went nuts over a rodeo clown.

The rodeo clown was performing at the Missouri State Fair, and he had the awful temerity to wear a mask of then-President Obama. "We're going to stomp Obama now," said an announcer. "Hey, I know I'm a clown," the rodeo clown replied. "He's just running around acting like one. Doesn't know he is one." The media quoted a bystander who compared the act to a Ku Klux Klan rally. The lieutenant governor of the state condemned the act, as did one of the senators. The rodeo clown was fired, even though he'd dressed up as other presidents in the past.

Fast-forward four years.

On Tuesday, TMZ posted photos of comedienne Kathy Griffin, who has helped host CNN's New Year's Eve coverage for a decade, holding a mock-up of President Trump's severed head covered in blood. Griffin has a long record of anti-Trump sentiment, of course; in February, she told MSNBC's Chris Matthews: "I'm a big resister, and I don't believe in compromise with this president. I also think he's crazy. I think he's mentally ill. He's also an idiot." But this photo shoot crossed a rather obvious line—it celebrated Trump's prospective murder. Imagine if anyone on the right had done something similar with Obama. The outcry would have been deafening.

Yet the same people who ask for trigger warnings for material that might offend anyone; the same people who believe that there is a "rape culture" that pervades America; the same people who say that President Trump has incentivized a culture of political violence across the land; are largely silent about Griffin's antics. Why? Because political violence is no longer taboo in the United States. It's just another tactic to utilize when useful and denigrate when others engage in it.

That sentiment expresses itself on both sides of the political aisle. When Montana House candidate Greg Gianforte allegedly body-slammed a reporter, prominent conservatives including talk-show host Laura Ingraham demeaned his victim as a wuss and championed Gianforte as a sort of stalwart man's man. When leftists attacked Trump rallies during the 2016 election cycle, the media attempted to paint them as defenders of the common good against Trump himself.

The overused phrase "cycle of violence" is often used by the press to refer to situations in which an aggressor acts violently and somebody defends him. But we've entered an actual cycle in violent political rhetoric, whereby the vileness of the left provokes a direct response from the right, and vice versa.

And it's getting worse.

If you spend all day proclaiming that you're in a "civil war" with other Americans, that you're part of the "resistance," it's only a matter of time until you become willing to look the other way at violence itself. If Americans aren't your brothers and sisters, if we disagree, then they will quickly become your enemies. Kathy Griffin may think it's hilarious to hold up a bloody head of the president of the United States, but she's tearing away at the social fabric far more than President Trump. And those who back her play are helping to provoke their enemies to respond in kind.

The Unbridgeable Gap Between Left and Right Over Human Evil

June 7, 2017

There are certain clarifying moments in political discourse; moments that demonstrate just where the various parties stand. Never has the gap been so obvious as this last week. On Friday, the left declared the world in imminent peril. The problem? President Trump pulled out of the altogether meaningless Paris climate accord, a worldwide agreement requesting nonbinding commitments from signatories about future carbon emissions cuts. The hysteria was palpable. Suddenly, debunked weather prognosticator Al Gore found himself in prime television slots jabbering about the end of the world. House Minority Leader Nancy Pelosi gabbled about how Trump was "dishonoring" God (no word on her abortion-on-demand position from the Holy One—blessed be he). The Huffington Post ran a headline showing the world in flames. The mayor of London, Sadiq Khan, released a statement bemoaning Trump's decision.

Meanwhile, the right shrugged. It pointed out that the agreement did virtually nothing anyway; that it did not bind China and India to any serious commitments; that the Senate had not passed any enabling legislation; and that perhaps nongovernment alternatives should be considered before diving headlong into empowerment of the regulatory state to fight a rising temperature over the next century.

On Saturday, a group of Islamic terrorists drove a van into a crowd on the London Bridge, and then jumped out of the vehicle and began stabbing people in surrounding establishments. The Islamic State group claimed responsibility. The right immediately labeled the attacks yet another example of Islamic extremism on the march, linking them with the Manchester terror attack. President Trump immediately took to Twitter to denounce the terror attacks and call for an end to politically correct policies, as well as to stump for his travel ban. Conservatives on both sides of the Atlantic complained about leftist multiculturalism creating room for Islamic terror growth.

Meanwhile, the left shrugged. Sally Kohn tweeted about the glories of political correctness. Paul Krugman compared being killed in a terrorist attack to being killed by a drunk driver. Democrats complained about President Trump's attacks on Khan, who was busy urging Londoners to stay calm after panicking about global warming just days ago.

What explains the gap between right and left?

The left believes that human beings are inherently good, and that only environment defines whether they will act in evil fashion. That's why Sen. Bernie Sanders articulated in 2016 that global warming was the spur to terrorism; it's why the Obama administration routinely suggested that poverty caused terrorism. External circumstances dictate the morality of individual actors. That's also why the left argues we shouldn't hold people responsible for their actions as a general rule; instead, we should reshape society.

The right believes that human beings are capable of evil on their own. That's why they see the rise of radical Islam as more of a problem than global warming. Good people won't kill each other because of global warming. They will if they begin to believe evil ideologies, or support those who do.

This gap isn't bridgeable. It goes to the nature of humanity and our perception of that nature. But it's requiring a greater and greater strain these days to blame anybody but individual human beings in free Western societies for their own descent into evil.

Trump Didn't Ruin the Media. Obama Did

June 14, 2017

There is a widespread perception among those on the right that President Trump's myriad foibles, vagaries and outright prevarications are somehow justifiable because he is The Great Destroyer of the mainstream media. His fans say he is running the media around in circles—and that is its own reward. Are you still waiting for extreme vetting? For the border wall? For tax cuts, Obamacare repeal and a massive military buildup? Well, sit down and shut up. Just be grateful that Trump has the media hysterically following his tweets like a hormonal teenage boy frantically searching for internet pornography.

But this is wrong.

Trump isn't destroying the media's credibility. They already destroyed their own credibility, thanks to their allegiance to President Barack Obama.

Trump has the benefit of occupying the presidency after Obama. The media was highly critical of President Bill Clinton—even they couldn't ignore the juicy scandals dripping daily from the White House in the 1990s. They were even more critical of President George W. Bush—they were more than willing to misreport in order to undermine a war and destroy a presidency.

But then came Obama.

Obama was the first indicator that the media would simply refuse to cover stories they didn't like about a politician they did. The media covered Clinton's Chinagate and Travelgate. But they refused to cover the IRS scandal with the same level of vim as they would have under Bush; they downplayed the Obama administration's involvement in the botched "Fast and Furious" gun operation scandal; and members of the mainstream media openly mocked the right's anger over the administration's manipulation of the 2012 Benghazi terror attack. Obama had to be protected at all costs, including the cost of the media's credibility.

Meanwhile, the media savaged 2012 Republican presidential nominee Mitt Romney. They dug up a story from his high school days regarding him forcibly cutting a classmate's hair. They uncovered scandalous material about him strapping a dog to the roof of his car. They delved deep into his nefarious practice of investing in failing companies, and then cutting the dead weight to turn them around.

Then came Trump.

Trump didn't do anything aside from failing to comply with media's standards of behavior. He didn't pander to them or treat them with respect. And the media melted down. They treated Trump horribly, of course—but they'd already treated Bush and Romney just as badly. More importantly, the media lost their ability to pretend having standards of honesty and decency after selling their souls to the Obama White House. It was difficult to take their cries of incipient tyranny seriously after they bent over backward to flatter a White House that cracked down on reporters from Fox News and the Associated Press.

Why does any of this matter?

It matters because conservatives would be wise to understand that Trump didn't destroy the media; he inherited the shell of a media ready to crumble. He tapped the shell, and it fell apart. But that's not enough. Trump now has a golden opportunity to promulgate an alternative narrative in place of the one pushed by the discredited leftist media—if he can demonstrate credibility himself.

So far, he hasn't. And that means that his credibility will crumble at first contact from someone who hasn't already destroyed his or her credibility. Hence the media's renewed love for former FBI Director James Comey—they believe that they can restore their own credibility by watching him destroy Trump's.

Trump can do significant damage to the media, but only if he tells the truth. Now would be an excellent time to start.

On 'Muh Principles'

June 21, 2017

"Muh principles."

It's a phrase we hear over and over on Twitter whenever someone criticizes morally troubling anti-leftist tactics used by members of the right. They say: "What are you, some sort of coward? What, are you worried about muh principles?" The phrase is meant to deride the supposed moral preening of those who criticize—they must think themselves high and mighty, whining about virtue where some good hard-nosed old-fashioned get-in-the-dirt-and-fight-'em tactics would do. Those worries about right and wrong just hamstring the right. "Muh principles" are a liability. Why can't those weaklings just get over their supposed moral purity and fight in the trenches?

Now, I'm no fan of political cowardice. I wrote an entire book called "Bullies," in which I blasted the left's character assassination techniques. I routinely speak on college campuses in conditions that are less than physically secure. I'm more than happy to tell people things they don't want to hear in political debate, and I've been threatened more than once for my trouble.

But I'm a fan of principles.

I'm a fan of principles because without them, politics becomes meaningless. Even those who criticize "muh principles" have their own principles. The "muh principles" crowd's highest principle is supposedly defeating the left. That is its entire argument: If you stick with your wishy-washy principles about civility, you'll lose! And if you lose, my principles will be destroyed!

But, as it turns out, many of those who mock "muh principles" have no actual principles other than empty tribal victory. Never was that clearer than this week when several of the self-appointed members of the Trump-ardent defense squad went full social justice warrior, invading a Shakespeare in the Park performance of "Julius Caesar" that depicts President Trump as Caesar. Screaming "Liberal hate kills!" they stormed the stage, called audience members Joseph Goebbels and held up the production. Those who objected to this obtuse behavior were simply being hamstrung by "muh principles," they then proclaimed.

Except that there were no principles at stake here. What was the supposed principle? Perhaps it was that artists shouldn't make art that invokes images of violence inflicted on a president. Then why weren't they upset about a rodeo clown dressed up as President Obama in 2013? Perhaps it was that radical rhetoric leads to violence. Then why weren't they upset when candidate Trump urged his followers to clock protesters? Perhaps it was that shutting down others' free speech is bad—a sort of ironic lesson for the left. Then why didn't they say so, rather than claiming that the content of the play justified their activity? And why would this be a good strategy, given that the self-immolating hard left's free speech shutdowns have backfired so dramatically that even Obama and Sens. Elizabeth Warren and Bernie Sanders have been forced to condemn them?

No, there were no principles here, other than tribalistic anti-left foolishness.

Unfortunately, that seems to be the order of the day for a few on the right. I'm old enough to remember when the pro-Trump right justified Trump's behavior on the grounds that he had to build a wall and rescind Obama's executive amnesty. Now only Ann Coulter has the guts to point out that Trump hasn't done either—and that he just enshrined for all time Obama's executive amnesty. I'm old enough to remember when the pro-Trump right assured conservatives that it would hold Trump to account if he were to fail to repeal Obamacare. Now it's ignoring the fact that he called a watered-down Obamacare too "mean" and pushed for a broader funding regime. Where are their principles? I thought "muh principles" had to go so that they could achieve theirs. But they seem rather blithe about the collapse of some of their supposed core precepts, which suggests that maybe there are some on the right who just want to fight, and have forgotten why they fight—and how to fight. All that matters now is winning, even if they have no idea what winning looks like other than the other guy losing.

But Reality Isn't Fair

June 28, 2017

In 2014, I debated Seattle City Council member and avowed socialist Kshama Sawant. Sawant was one of the chief proponents of a city ordinance that would create a $15 minimum wage. Eventually, the city adopted a three-phase transition plan that would push minimum wage to $11 per hour, then $13 per hour, then $15 per hour. In our debate, I asked Sawant directly whether she would support a $1,000 minimum wage. She deflected the question, of course. She deflected the question because reality would not allow for a $1,000 minimum wage. Were the government to mandate such an idiocy, every business in the Seattle area would immediately cut back employment, and all of those seeking minimum wage jobs would end up losing their income.

As it turns out, it didn't take a $1,000 minimum wage to destroy the income for minimum wage workers. Thirteen dollars was plenty. According to a paper from The National Bureau of Economic Research, "the minimum wage ordinance lowered low-wage employees' earnings by an average of $125 per months in 2016."

All of this was foreseeable, given the fact that businesses compete with one another to lower cost and thus operate with slim profit margins. That means businesses have two choices when government forcibly raises labor costs: increase prices and thereby lower demand, or cut back on the work force. Businesses opted to do the latter in order to stay competitive.

Reality is unpleasant. Perhaps that's why so few politicians seem willing to face up to it.

On a larger scale, the bipartisan consensus in favor of regulations that force insurance companies to cover pre-existing conditions mirrors the minimum wage debate. It is perfectly obvious that forcing insurance companies—professional risk assessors that determine pricing based on actuarial estimates as to health—to cover those with pre-existing conditions costs them an enormous amount of money. If you are a consumer, why would you bother buying a health insurance plan while healthy, when you could wait to do so until after your costs materialize? Yet both parties would rather cater to the foolish notion that it is "unfair" for insurance companies to act as insurance companies than allow insurance companies to do what they do best: create a market to allow Americans to exercise choice.

But in economics, once one heresy has been advanced, a slew of other heresies follow. Coverage of pre-existing conditions has to be subsidized somehow. Democrats propose to mandate that people buy health insurance; this violates freedom of choice and artificially increases premiums for the healthy in order to pay for the sick. Republicans propose subsidies to encourage purchase, artificially creating demand without allowing the competition among health plans that would keep premiums down.

But everyone is surprised when such schemes fail.

They shouldn't be. Politics used to be the art of educating the public about reality and pushing for change where change is possible. Now politics is the art of convincing the public that you can make reality disappear if it votes for you. Sadly, our politicians can't make reality disappear.

Does Being Presidential Matter Anymore?

July 5, 2017

It's tempting to view President Trump as the end of the American presidential tradition. It's difficult to imagine George Washington pondering a future president of the United States tweeting out memes of himself clotheslining a CNN-logoed enemy. It would certainly confuse Abraham Lincoln to see the president jabbering about media enemies' bloody face-lifts and then declaring himself "modern day presidential." On moving into the White House, John Adams wrote to his wife, Abigail Adams, "May none but honest and wise Men ever rule under this roof."

Yeah, not so much.

But while the media act as though Trump is a shocking break from his predecessors, the fact is that they took the first steps down the path of merging the frivolous and the grave. They began violating public standards long before Trump was ever a presidential contender. Trump defenders aren't wrong to scoff at Bill Clinton supporters suddenly discovering presidential propriety two decades after defending their favorite's cigar tricks with a White House intern in the Oval Office. And Barack Obama wasn't exactly shy about making the media rounds in the most ridiculous way—it was he, after all, who began appearing with GloZell and Pimp With the Limp in order to press forward his political case.

But Trump is indeed something new. He doesn't even pretend to be presidential. Clinton failed at being presidential, but he still *wanted* to be seen as a serious human being; Obama tried to position himself as a serious thinker, even as he did his latest ESPN brackets. Trump has no such pretentions—or if he does, his volatile id won't allow him to stick to them. He's open and obvious about his disdain for decency and protocol. He spends his days trolling Reddit and 4chan for the latest dank memes to post to his Twitter account, and then he waits with bated breath as his followers cheer themselves hoarse.

So, does any of this matter?

It's tempting to say that it doesn't. George W. Bush attempted to restore some honor to the office after Clinton spread his bodily juices all over it. The media savaged him anyway, and called him a nincompoop and a dunce and a humiliation to the office. Obama entered on eagle's wings and promptly used the bully pulpit to attack his enemies and cover for his friends. What difference does it make whether Trump finally strips the mask off the hoity-toity old boys club that the White House represents?

Actually, it does make a difference.

It makes a difference because while we're always going to have the rough-and-tumble of politics—and we *should*, because we live in a free country—there's a whole generation of Americans who have been gradually acclimated to bad behavior by their leaders. Clinton started us down a dark path. Trump stands at the end of the path, thanks, ironically, to the public's distaste for the Clintons. Trump could have helped restore a sense of honor to the White House. He didn't. It's possible in theory that such a failure could help Americans turn to a sort of small-government libertarianism and say to themselves, "Hey, why give these dolts a bunch of power?" Instead, Americans seem to be saying to themselves: "Hey, why do the other guys get to be awful? Why can't we do it, too?"

The result: a race to the bottom. That race seems to be accelerating daily now. Again, that's not Trump's fault. It's ours. We ought to demand that our politicians be more than celebrities who enjoy WWE memes or Hollywood-adored figureheads for "woke" talking points. They ought to act out some sort of honor in their Constitutional roles. It's enough to churn the stomach to imagine the great people who once occupied the halls of power, and then consider what moral Lilliputians now roam there.

What If There's No
Trump-Putin Conspiracy?

July 12, 2017

This week, The New York Times dropped a potential bombshell: It alleged that Donald Trump Jr., then-Trump presidential campaign manager Paul Manafort and President Trump's son-in-law, Jared Kushner, met with a Russian government-linked lawyer in order to hear potential dirt about Hillary Clinton. The media immediately declared victory—this was obviously the first step toward establishing the Trump-Russia collusion about which they have crowed for nearly a year.

Meanwhile, Trump issued a series of tweets implying that he created a relationship of trust with Russian President Vladimir Putin, and that he might consider the foundation of a joint cybersecurity "unit" with the regime that allegedly attempted to influence the American election.

All of this looks rather suspicious, unless it turns out that pretty much every Trumpian scandal can be explained through a combination of Trump's ego and the incompetence of those around him.

Here's the truth: Even if every allegation surrounding Trump Jr., Manafort and Kushner regarding this meeting is true, that's *still* not evidence of any working relationship between the Trump campaign and the Russian government. At best, it's evidence that Trump Jr. and Co. weren't averse to attempts to feed them information. But as all accounts of the meeting state, no actual information was transferred, which means that there's *still* no Trump-Russia collusion.

What of Trump's bizarre behavior regarding Putin? The most obvious explanation isn't nefarious manipulation but pure, old-fashioned spite. Trump feels assaulted by the media who have been accusing him of being a Putin puppet since mid-2016. Rather than distancing himself from Putin, Trump's initial tendency is always to "punch back 10 times harder," as Melania Trump put it. That means embracing Putin, demonstrating a nonchalant apathy toward rumors and even treating Putin as a potential partner—after all, he has treated Trump more nicely than the media accusing him of corruption. From an egocentric perspective, Trump has more in common with Putin than he does with CNN.

That may be ugly, but it's also not collusion. It's not even in the same ballpark as then-President Obama promising "flexibility" to the Russians before the 2012 election.

This leaves the media short of the kill shot they've been implicitly promising for months. Ant that, in turn, makes the media desperate to prove that this hasn't all been a waste of time, a perverse attempt to find conspiracies in alphabet soup. And that means overplaying every single story into the Harbinger of Doom.

Here's the truth: Trump isn't a conspiratorial mastermind. He's a man irked by empty criticisms and dedicated to kicking his enemies in their most vulnerable areas. Sometimes that looks like he's reinforcing their theories. He isn't. So long as the media insist that Trump is someone he isn't, they'll keep finding conspiracies that don't fit the facts or the personality.

Yes, Politics Is Dirty. No, It Isn't As Dirty As You Think It Is

July 19, 2017

Expectations define behavior.

The success of a marriage nearly always depends on the expectations of the parties going in. If you believe marriage is going to be a rose garden of happy trips to the beach interspersed with moonlight dinners and foot massages, you're more likely to end up cheating on your spouse when that doesn't materialize. If you believe marriage is a mechanism for changing your potential spouse, you're likely to end up estranged. If you believe that marriage is about a lifelong union devoted to self-improvement and the creation and rearing of children, you're likely to make decisions that lead to that outcome.

The same is true in politics.

Americans don't trust politicians. That's for good reason. Politicians fib to get elected; they pander to particular constituencies; they leave principle at the door in favor of convenience in order to maintain power and position. But they do not, at least not that often, murder people and collude with foreign governments.

But thanks to popular culture, that's exactly what many Americans think politicians do. If you watch "House of Cards," you're likely to believe that top-level politicians off each other on a regular basis—and you might be more willing to believe conspiracy theories about the murder of former Democratic National Committee staffer Seth Rich. If you've seen "The Manchurian Candidate," you're more likely to believe that either former President Obama or President Trump is one.

President Trump, who was a layman until he became president, obviously believes a lot of the pop culture mythology surrounding politics. That's why he told Bill O'Reilly that it's not that big a deal that Russian President Vladimir Putin kills his political opponents. "You think our country's so innocent?" he said in jaw-dropping fashion. That's why Trump believes that politics is such a "dirty business"—dirtier, even, than Manhattan real estate, where Trump worked with mafia figures. Politics, in Trump's mind, is the lowest of the low.

That means a more corrupt administration. If you believe, as Trump assuredly does, that anybody would take a meeting with Russian government figures to dig up dirt on an opponent, then you'll do it, too. Why be martyred just because you were too holy to get down in the mud? If you think that Hillary Clinton is the way politics is done—we shouldn't be outraged because she's just another politician—then why not play by the same rules?

Voters like to believe, as Trump does, that politics is filthy, because we refuse to acknowledge that in a representative republic, we're the ultimate sources of blame. We keep electing these moral idiots. We keep voting for them, demanding that they give us things and suggesting that they've "sold out" if they don't. We're the ones who decry crony capitalism while complaining that the local factory will leave unless the government "does something."

Politicians like to believe, as Trump does, that politics is sordid, because that's a tailor-made excuse for participating in bad behavior. It's also an excuse for legislating morality, as Sen. John McCain tried to do with campaign finance reform—you can use the public distrust of politicians to restrict the political speech of citizens, all in the name of "cleaning up the system."

It's always easier to shift our vision of politics than to shift our vision of ourselves.

And so, we get the politics we deserve. Our belief that politics is a squalid affair finds realization in our politicians, who reflect that view; and in ourselves, as we vote for those politicians. And then we're surprised when politics seems to grow more and more disreputable.

Why the Left Protects Islam

July 26, 2017

Richard Dawkins is no friend to conservatives. The atheist author has spent much of his life deriding Judaism and Christianity. He once stated, "An atheist is just somebody who feels about Yahweh the way any decent Christian feels about Thor or Baal or the golden calf." Dawkins says that even moderate religious people "make the world safe for extremists." He's far to the left on politics: He's pro-abortion rights, and a supporter of the Labour Party and the Liberal Democrats in Britain.

But he's also smart enough to recognize that radical Islam is a greater threat to human life than Christianity or Judaism. He explains: "I have criticised the appalling misogyny and homophobia of Islam, I have criticised the murdering of apostates for no crime other than their disbelief. ... Muslims themselves are the prime victims of the oppressive cruelties of Islamism."

Such language makes him a pariah among leftists.

This week, Dawkins was scheduled to speak at an event with KPFA radio in Berkeley, California. All went swimmingly—until leftists realized that Dawkins had said some untoward things about Islam. The station then canceled the event, citing his "abusive speech." It explained: "We had booked this event based entirely on his excellent new book on science, when we didn't know he had offended and hurt—in his tweets and other comments on Islam, so many people. KPFA does not endorse hurtful speech."

This is no shock. The same left that barred Dawkins from his Berkeley event cheered this week while Palestinian Arabs rioted over metal detectors at the Temple Mount. Those leftists proclaim that the true obstacle to peace in the Middle East isn't Palestinian

Arab violence—it isn't Palestinians who stab Israeli Druz officers on the Temple Mount; or the Palestinians who invade homes and slaughter old men and women; or the Palestinians in government who cheer, honor and financially support such behavior. No, the problem is the Jews.

The same left that blames metal detectors for murderous assaults and Richard Dawkins for offending Islam makes excuses for radical Muslim and Women's March on Washington organizer Linda Sarsour, who has called for certain apostate Muslims to have their genitals removed, says that Zionists cannot be feminists and stands up for terrorists and terror supporters.

Why does the left seek to support radical Islam so ardently? Because the left believes that the quickest way to destroy Western civilization is no longer class warfare but multicultural warfare: Simply ally with groups that hate the prevailing system and work with them to take it down. Then, the left will build on the ashes of the old system. In this view, Dawkins is an opponent—how can the left recruit Muslims to fight the system if Dawkins is busy alienating them? They support the Palestinian terror regime—how can that colonialist outpost, Israel, be defeated without a little blood? They applaud Sarsour—she's an ally, so she must be backed.

Alliance with nefarious forces calls your own morality into question. KPFA has a lot more to answer for than Dawkins. But the left will never have to answer such questions so long as it focuses in on its common enemy: a supposedly conservative establishment that must be fought with any tool at its disposal.

Instability Is Not Unpredictability

August 2, 2017

One of the great myths about President Trump is that America's enemies would fear him because he is predictably unpredictable. Trump himself stated during the campaign that he didn't want to spell out general military strategy because he didn't want to warn our enemies. "Douglas MacArthur, George Patton spinning in their graves when they see the stupidity of our country," he stated during one of his debates with Hillary Clinton. And in April 2016, he stated: "We are totally predictable. We tell everything. We're sending troops? We tell them. We're sending something else? We have a news conference. We have to be unpredictable, and we have to be unpredictable starting now."

Trump, the theory went, would certainly be unpredictable.

The theory gained credibility after Trump decided to fire a missile at a Syrian airbase in the aftermath of American intelligence reporting that Syrian President Bashar Assad decided to use weapons of mass destruction on Syrian civilians. It seemed he had the capacity to frighten our enemies—you never know what might set him off. That was a *good* thing: It left those who would challenge us in the dark as to where his triggers would be. If North Korean leader Kim Jong Un were to go too far, he might find himself on the wrong end of a cruise missile.

Now, it seems, Trump isn't unpredictable. He's absolutely predictable. He's just unstable.

There's a difference between unpredictability and instability. Unpredictability can be strategic. It can allow you to shift your moves in order to throw off your opposition. It means shifting your actual strategy and sticking with that new strategy. It's a key component of any chess game: Do something different and throw your opponent off course.

Instability is different. Instability typically manifests as shocking initial action followed by utterly predictable regression to the norm. The unstable people you know may flare up occasionally, but they generally settle down in relatively short order. And we can often predict *when* they will become unstable: when they feel threatened, when they have an emotional response to something out of the ordinary.

That seems more like Trump.

His initial bursts of rage generally peter out until convenience dictates action. If there's any massive blowback at all, he backs off. That's why his treatment of Attorney General Jeff Sessions is actually damaging to America on foreign policy: It leads our enemies to believe they can willfully ignore Trump's initial fulminations and then bet on cooler heads to prevail. It's not a coincidence that Russia and North Korea are gradually upping the ante with Trump in the belief that Trump will talk tough and do little.

All of this means that Trump may have to do something truly unpredictable: take a hard stand. On the home front, that means restructuring his administration so that it looks more like a major corporation than a family business, with rules and chains of command. We can hope and pray that retired Gen. John Kelly provides some of that structure. On the foreign policy front, Trump will have to stand behind real consequences for bad actors.

If Trump continues to respond to situations with knee-jerk activity followed by grudging acceptance, he won't live up to the promise he made: to unleash hell, in unpredictable but effective fashion, on the enemies of the United States should they violate our interests.

Google's Leftist Goggles
Leave Googlers Agog

August 9, 2017

So, Google is a leftist company.

That's no surprise. All you'd have to do to verify that fact is watch the rotating Google doodles throughout the year. They frequently feature social justice warriors, leftist causes celebres and random slaps at religion. Or you could check its search results, which tend to favor leftist causes and politicians over conservative ones.

But Google isn't just liberal; it's leftist. It's so leftist that its vice president of Diversity, Integrity & Governance, Danielle Brown, participated in a public scourging of an unnamed Google employee who had the temerity to question the company's odd focus on "diversity" hires. The employee penned a 10-page Jerry Maguire-style memo outlining Google's obsession with "diversity" and why its practices amount to illegal discrimination—and pointing out that the lack of women in top positions reflects scientific differences between men and women on average, not discriminatory social policy.

This intrepid soul openly signaled his opposition to sexism but then pointed out that personality differences between men and women on average, as well as men's higher drive for status, could lead to wage gaps at the company. That is absolutely correct based on a tremendous amount of available social science data. In fact, it's also true that while women on average may slightly outperform men on IQ tests, more men are found at the extremes of the bell curve—there are more men on the upper and lower ends of the spectrum.

That would lead to the hiring of more men at prestigious companies like Google based on merit, not based on sexism.

But according to Google itself, such wrongthink must be curbed. And so, Brown stated that the memo "advanced incorrect assumptions about gender." Not controversial—incorrect. The facts, you see, must be made to fit Google's theory. Furthermore, said Brown, "I'm not going to link to it here as it's not a viewpoint that I or this company endorses." But there was good news. "Diversity and inclusion are a fundamental part of our values and the culture we continue to cultivate," she said.

Yay, diversity! Shut up, guy who disagrees!

Unfortunately, this philosophy of diversity before freedom or merit has run amok at many of America's major companies. And it has an impact on product. YouTube has reportedly been restricting videos it deems controversial or inappropriate, and disproportionately targeting comics like Steven Crowder and educators like Dennis Prager. Facebook has taken steps in recent months to curb its own biases, but only after a blowup with conservatives who were angry at its apparent attempts to crack down on non-leftists. Twitter has banned or suspended conservatives for mysterious reasons that it has never applied to members of the left.

Google has a pair of leftist goggles on at all times. Its users shouldn't have blinders on about it. Every search result should be scanned for algorithmic bias. After all, a company that will rip its own employee to shreds for defending its hiring practices on the basis of science and data will do anything to defend its leftist politics.

The Group That Got Ignored in Charlottesville

August 16, 2017

The "alt-right" is evil. White supremacism is evil. Neo-Nazism is evil.

I've been saying these things my entire career; I've spent more than a year slamming various factions on the right that refuse to disassociate from and condemn popularizers of the racist alt-right. The media, too, have spent inordinate time covering the rise of the alt-right and tacit acquiescence to it from White House chief strategist Steve Bannon and President Trump. So when an alt-right piece of human debris drove a car at 40 mph into a crowd of protesters in Charlottesville, Virginia, last Saturday, injuring 19 people and killing a 32-year-old woman, the level of scrutiny on the alt-right forced Trump to condemn various alt-right groups by name.

Good.

But the media have remained largely silent about another group: Antifa. Antifa is a loosely connected band of anti-capitalist protesters generally on the far left who dub themselves "anti-fascist" after their compatriots in Europe. They've been around in the United States since the 1990s, protesting globalization and burning trash cans at World Trade Organization meetings. But they've kicked into high gear over the past two years: They engaged in vandalism in violence, forcing the cancelation of a speech by alt-right popularizer Milo Yiannopoulos at the University of California, Berkeley; a few months later, they attacked alt-right demonstrators in Berkeley; they attacked alt-right demonstrators in Sacramento, California, leading to a bloody street fight; they threw projectiles at police during

President Trump's inauguration; they attacked pro-Trump free-speech demonstrators in Seattle last weekend. They *always* label their opponents "fascists" in order to justify their violence.

In Charlottesville, Antifa engaged in street violence with the alt-right racists. As in Weimar, Germany, fascists flying the swastika engaged in hand-to-hand combat with Antifa members flying the communist red. And yet, the media declared that any negative coverage granted to Antifa would detract from the obvious evils of the alt-right. Sheryl Gay Stolberg of The New York Times tweeted in the midst of the violence, "The hard left seemed as hate-filled as alt-right. I saw club-wielding 'antifa' beating white nationalists being led out of the park." After receiving blowback from the left, Stolberg then corrected herself. She said: "Rethinking this. Should have said violent, not hate-filled. They were standing up to hate."

Or perhaps Antifa is a hateful group itself. But that wouldn't fit the convenient narrative Antifa promotes and the media buy: that the sole threat to the republic comes from the racist right. Perhaps that's why the media ignored the events in Sacramento and Berkeley and Seattle—to point out the evils of Antifa might detract from the evils of the alt-right.

That sort of biased coverage only engenders more militancy from the alt-right, which feels it must demonstrate openly and repeatedly to "stand up to Antifa." Which, of course, prompts Antifa to violence.

Here's the moral solution, as always: Condemn violence and evil wherever it occurs. The racist philosophy of the alt-right is evil. The violence of the alt-right is evil. The communist philosophy of Antifa is evil. So is the violence of Antifa. If we are to survive as a republic, we must call out Nazis but not punch them; we must stop providing cover to anarchists and communists who seek to hide behind self-proclaimed righteousness to participate in violence. Otherwise, we won't be an honest or a free society.

President Trump and the
Politics of Attitude

August 23, 2017

Last week, President Trump ousted his White House chief strategist, Steve Bannon. Bannon was widely perceived as a divisive figure—a self-promoting rabid political attack dog dedicated to "winning" at all costs; a fellow who declared the website he used to run, Breitbart, a forum for the "alt-right." To put it mildly, Bannon wasn't well-liked. For months, he had been living on borrowed time at the White House and was marginalized by Trump in favor of now-chief of staff John Kelly, national security adviser H.R. McMaster, and senior advisers Jared Kushner and Ivanka Trump, among others.

Bannon's firing caused a bit of a firestorm on the right, particularly after Bannon stated that "The Trump presidency that we fought for, and won, is over." He meant that Trump's allegiance to "nationalist populism" was over—that Trump was now surrounded by Democrats and generals.

But here's the truth: Trump's nationalist-populist presidency never truly began. Trump was hailed by his allies as a transformative figure, the leader of a new kind of movement centered not around conservatism but around pragmatism. According to Bannon, this meant trillion-dollar infrastructure packages and hardcore tariffs; it meant pulling out of Afghanistan and raising taxes on the rich. It also meant a border wall. Bannon was one of a cadre of would-be philosophers attempting to cobble Trumpism into something coherent.

But none of those things were happening before Bannon left. Trump was never an ideologue or a pragmatist. He was—and is—a bundle of attitudes. Americans are either attracted to those attitudes or repelled by them. They include the need to punch back as hard as possible at perceived enemies; an unwillingness to study issues in any sort of depth, because experts are merely eggheads; a focus on imaging, particularly as it pertains to him personally; and a knee-jerk animus against those who would insult institutions. All of this makes the Trump administration confused and confusing.

It also means that the best conservative hopes for a Trump administration lie not in the cheerleading of sites like Breitbart, or the manipulations of House Speaker Paul Ryan, R-Wis., or Senate Majority Leader Mitch McConnell, R-Ky., but with Democrats. If Democrats were smart, they'd see that Trump has already been alienated by conservatives and "nationalist populists"—that he's in search of an emotional home. They'd begin cultivating him; they'd push him to sign broad bipartisan legislation.

But, like Trump, the Democratic Party is more of a collections of attitudes than policies. And its primary attitude is animus for Trump personally. That means it'll forgo any gain in order to slap Trump. So in order to drive Trump's approval ratings lower, Democrats will continue to avoid working with him like he's the plague.

What comes next? The most probable answer: not much. That's not because of Bannon or the Democrats. It's because of Trump. When it comes to governing, ideology matters; philosophy matters. Attitude only matters when it comes to getting elected. President Trump is finding that out day by day. So are some of his most ardent and passionate ideological supporters.

What Hurricane Harvey Teaches Us About Humanity

August 30, 2017

The pictures, videos and social media posts coming out of Houston, Texas, thanks to Hurricane Harvey are horrifying: children camped out on kitchen counters in order to avoid flooding; elderly women stuck in rest homes and up to their waist in water; tweets from local police departments reminding residents to bring axes into their attic in case they have to cut their way through their roof to escape rising waters. But just as many pictures and videos are inspirational: local men and women hopping into their boats and looking for victims to rescue; police carrying children out of flooded houses; Americans helping one another.

Whenever disaster strikes, we're always inspired by images of human beings helping one another. Disaster often brings out the best in us: our capacity for care, our bravery in risking our lives to help others. Then we're inevitably disappointed in our unending ability to leave those qualities behind the moment disaster ends. We'll rush into burning buildings to save each other, but we'll club each other on the head at political rallies.

Why?

Because there are certain enemies we hold in common. We hold death in common; we'll help all but our worst enemies escape the grave. We hold natural disasters in common as an enemy; we'll react to them by helping out our neighbors. And we hold civilizational threats in common; we'll fight together against the Nazi scourge or the Soviet threat.

But what about when there is no civilizational threat? What about when we're so powerful that serious threats seem unserious? Former President Obama informed us routinely that radical Islamic terrorism didn't threaten our civilization. It's no wonder, then, that so few Americans see radical Islam as a threat worth unifying against. President Trump tells us that Russia isn't a civilizational threat, and neither is global warming. Without a credible existential threat, Americans don't unify.

But there is a credible existential threat to Americans. The problem is that it's internal.

America was built on the foundation of free speech, liberty in personal action, and freedom from violence and governmental tyranny. Those principles are now under attack by groups like antifa, far-left-leaning militants, which maintains that there *is* an existential threat that justifies wartime measures: the presence of the American system itself. Antifa members believe America is steeped in racism, bigotry, economic injustice and police barbarity. And they believe that this gives them the right to carve away at the foundations that hold us together.

This makes them an existential threat, a cancer gnawing at the vitals of the nation. They aren't the only ones, of course: Some violent members of the "alt-right," for example, believe that non-white Americans are the existential threat and use the same logic as antifa. But the true threat to America comes not from outside but from within. It's far harder to unify against that threat if we're unwilling to identify it.

But we should be willing to unify. We should all be willing to defend our neighbors in the peaceful expression of their rights—we should stand with them against violence. We should commit acts of kindness and heroism to help them. There is a storm coming. We must fight it together, or it will overwhelm us while we close our eyes to its danger.

If Republicans Don't Make a Move, They Deserve to Lose

September 6, 2017

Politics is the art of shifting the playing field.

This is an art Republicans simply don't understand. Perhaps it's because they spend so much time attempting to stop the Democratic snowball from running downhill too quickly, but Republicans in power have an unfortunate tendency to conserve their political capital rather than invest it. That's unfortunate because political capital doesn't accrue when you save it; it degrades. Just as sticking your cash in a mattress is a bad strategy when it comes to investment, inaction in power is a bad strategy when it comes to politics.

Democrats understand that political capital must be used, not to pass popular legislation but to fundamentally change the nature of the political game itself. Democrats do not see Obamacare—a piece of legislation that cost them the House, the Senate and, eventually, the presidency—as a disaster area. They see it as an investment in a leftist future: By making Americans accustomed to the idea that the government is responsible for universal coverage, they understand that any future failures will be attributed to lack of government, not an excess of it. Sen. Ted Cruz, R-Texas, understood that in 2013 when he attempted to block Obamacare funding. He quite rightly explained that once Obamacare went into effect, it would be nearly impossible to dismantle it. That became obvious this year, just four years after its full implementation, when congressional Republicans obviously have no political will to get rid of Obamacare at all.

This is the difference between Republicans and Democrats: Democrats see their radical legislative moves as building blocks for the future. Republicans, afraid that their carefully crafted tower of electability will come crumbling down, make no radical legislative moves.

That basic formula is playing out yet again with regard to former President Obama's executive amnesty. Obama implemented the Deferred Action for Childhood Arrivals program, or DACA, knowing full well that a Republican president could get rid of it with the stroke of a pen. But he also knew that Republicans would not want to be responsible for changing the status quo—they wouldn't want to own the political consequences of allowing the deportation of DACA recipients.

And Obama was completely right. Republicans promised for years that they would get rid of Obama's executive amnesty if given power. Finally, President Trump has pledged to get rid of it ... in six months. And everyone knows that he is willing to trade away DACA enforcement for border-wall funding. The Democratic status quo will win out, one way or another.

Now, quickly: Name the last transformational *conservative* change Republicans have made—a change to the field of play; any change that would redound to the detriment of Democrats. It's pretty tough. That's despite Republican control of the legislature and the presidency from 2002 to 2006; that's a longer period of unified control than Democrats had from 2008 to 2010.

Republicans have unified control of government once again. But they seem less willing to use it than ever, afraid that their tenuous control will dissipate.

That must end. If Republicans hope to set a foundation for future victory, they'll need to do more than act as an impediment to bad Democratic ideas. They'll need to take political risks in order to shift the playing field itself. If they don't, they'll lose quickly. And they'll deserve to lose.

Democrats' Newest Plan: Nationalized Health Care

September 13, 2017

On Monday, two seemingly unrelated headlines made the news. The first: America's national debt had finally reached $20 trillion. The second: New Jersey Democratic Sen. Cory Booker had finally come out in favor of Vermont independent Sen. Bernie Sanders' magical, mythical "Medicare-For-All" plan.

Of course, the two aren't unrelated at all. Once again, the Democratic Party is signing checks the country can't cash. Sanders' Medicare-For-All scheme would add some $13.8 trillion in spending over the first decade alone. Medicare already carries $58 trillion in unfunded liabilities, according to National Review. How unrealistic is Medicare-For-All? It's so unrealistic that the state of California has rejected a single-payer health care for being too expensive—and California currently has a Democratic supermajority in the state assembly.

Yet Democrats continue to push further and further to the left, fearful of being outflanked. Booker isn't alone in his newfound embrace of socialized medicine. California's Sen. Kamala Harris has also endorsed Sanders' ridiculous plan. Massachusetts Sen. Elizabeth Warren will be co-sponsoring Sanders' plan, as will Democratic Sen. Jeff Merkley of Oregon.

Why? Because Democrats are deeply frightened of being outflanked by socialists. There's no benefit to moving to the center when your base sees no purpose in fiscal responsibility. So instead, Democrats race one another to the Soviet Union.

Meanwhile, Republicans cower in fear. Afraid of making the case for freedom, they compete with Democrats to see who can administer the giant state more "efficiently," as though efficiency were the key problem with statism. Thus, Republicans ran headlong from the possibility of repealing Obamacare, afraid that the American people would backlash against them for "taking away" some form of entitlement.

This is a mistake by Republicans. Yes, whoever touches entitlements pays a price. But that's not true if the alternative is a slide into total governmental control. That's the case Republicans made from the day Obamacare was initiated: that it was the first step toward socialized medicine. Now Democrats are showing that the Republican critique was true. Republicans ought to provide a binary choice here: Either slide into nationalized health care with Democrats or help us tear away the bulwarks of tyranny in health care in favor of freedom.

In exposing their own radicalism, the Democrats have provided Republicans with an opportunity to seize the middle with conservatism. Republicans need not bend before the media's insistence that health care is a government responsibility—they can easily and honestly point at the Democratic frontrunners and identify the agenda. The question is whether Republicans have the courage to do so or whether they've bought the false narrative that President Trump won because he campaigned as a centrist. Trump won promising full Obamacare repeal. Republicans can do the same now and have the credibility of an awful alternative behind them.

All it takes is courage. Democratic cowardice has led the Party down the primrose path to full-on socialism. Now, Republicans must either make a stand against it or be complicit in bringing about that regime.

The End of the First Amendment

September 20, 2017

Last week, I visited the University of California, Berkeley.

The preparations for the visit were patently insane. First, the school charged the sponsor group, Young America's Foundation, a $15,000 security fee. Then, the school blocked off the upper level of the auditorium, fearful that radicals from the violent far-left-leaning group antifa would infiltrate the speech and begin hurling objects from the balcony onto the crowd below. Finally, the school ended up spending some $600,000 on additional policing, including the creation of cement barriers and hiring of hundreds of armed police officers for a prospective riot.

All this so that I could deliver a speech about personal responsibility and individualism.

Good for Berkeley for doing its job. Bad for the students and outside agitators who made it necessary. Unfortunately, the bad actors are becoming more prominent and more popular. At The University of Utah, we're already hearing rumors of unrest. And, according to an astonishing new survey from Brookings Institution, such idiocy is set to multiply: A full 44 percent of students said that the First Amendment does not protect "hate speech"; a majority of students, 51 percent, said that they would be in favor of students shouting down a speaker "known for making offensive and hurtful statements"; Nineteen percent of students said the use of violence against controversial speakers would be acceptable.

This is full-scale fascism, and it's gaining ground.

Meanwhile, administrators are caving. At Middlebury College, administrators have adopted a policy that explicitly states, "Only in cases of imminent and credible threat to the community that cannot be mitigated by revisions to the event plan would the president and senior administration consider canceling the event." At DePaul University, I was pre-emptively banned from campus last year after students got violent with another speaker. At the University of Wisconsin-Madison, police left students who decided to storm the stage while I was speaking to their own devices; administrators reportedly told the police not to remove the agitators and to cancel the event if they felt it necessary to do so. At California State University, Los Angeles, administrators allegedly told police to stand down rather than fight near-rioters getting violent with those who would attend one of my speeches.

Both students and administrators should take a lesson from Berkeley.

First, administrators: Security is necessary for the free exercise of the First Amendment. Right now, there's an expectation that police will be prevented from doing their jobs; that's why groups like antifa roam free. At Berkeley, they knew better: The police were armed with pepper spray and told to arrest anyone in a mask or with a barred weapon. The result was 1,000 protesters and no serious violence. That was after months of actual brutal violence in the streets of Berkeley. Other campuses must take note.

Second, students: Get a grip. I spoke at Berkeley without incident, and we actually had productive discussions with a number of students on the left. Everybody left with more information than they had coming in. Discussion never hurt anyone. But both the heckler's veto and the fascistic worldview that fuels it do.

The Strategy of Going Too Far

September 27, 2017

There's a running argument on the right these days. It begins each time the left overreacts to a Trumpian move with wild radicalism, alienating Americans in the middle. Some on the right attribute the left's penchant for political hara-kiri to President Donald Trump's masterful manipulations—it's just part of his genius. But the more plausible argument is that Trump isn't playing anyone—he's perfectly authentic. And most importantly, he always goes just a bit too far.

Going too far can be a political liability. But it can also tempt opponents into a game of chicken. And that's where Trump's hyperbolic approach to every issue sometimes redounds to his benefit. If Trump had stated last week in Alabama that he opposed former NFL quarterback Colin Kaepernick's brainless decision to kneel for the national anthem, he'd have been well in bounds. Instead, Trump went further. Channeling his old WWE/"The Apprentice" persona, he bellowed, "Wouldn't you love to see one of these NFL owners, when somebody disrespects our flag, to say, 'Get that son of a b—— off the field right now. Out. He's fired. He's fired!'"

The left leapt on Trump's over-the-line statements—and proceeded to land directly on a political land mine. Instead of ripping Trump for overstepping the boundaries of the presidency and talking about the necessity for preservation of First Amendment freedoms, the left called for widespread participation in kneeling. They couldn't merely side against Trump; they had to side with Kaepernick.

This, of course, was political idiocy. The vast majority of Americans think that kneeling during the national anthem is disrespectful, and that it represents a slap in the face to the military and the American flag. They think this because Kaepernick has explicitly said so: "I am not going to stand up to show pride in a flag for a country that oppresses black people and people of color." But prompted by a strategy of knee-jerk massive retaliation, the left decided to jump on board with Kaepernick anyway.

Meanwhile, Trump's own supporters saw nothing wrong with his statements—particularly once the left knelt with Kaepernick. Where some Trump supporters might have been tempted to say that Trump went too far, now they were more likely to back him—after all, he was speaking truth to those who would protest the flag.

All of which suggests that saying too much is actually a smart way to trigger your enemies and rally your base. President Obama knew this; it's undoubtedly why he made statements about Trayvon Martin looking like his fictional son. Sticking a fork in the eye of your enemy sometimes leads to your enemy blindly groping his way into the street, only to be mashed by the passing cars of political reality.

But none of this is good for a more rational politics. We should all be able to recognize that kneeling for the national anthem is foolishness, and that the president has no business calling for the firing of those in the private sector exercising First Amendment rights. That requires no overreach, and it doesn't make headlines. But it does create a unity sorely lacking in our politics.

The Power of Good

October 4, 2017

This week, an evil human being murdered nearly 60 Americans and wounded more than 500 others in Las Vegas. His attack was well-planned: The shooter had some 23 guns in his hotel room, including a semi-automatic rifle affixed with a "bump stock" allowing the shooter to operate the rifle like an automatic weapon; he had another 19 guns in his home. Video of the incident is chilling: the rat-a-tat of the gun raining bullets down on unsuspecting innocents from the hulking profile of the Mandalay Bay on the horizon, the wounded concertgoers screaming in the darkness.

But there was heroism, too.

The stranger who threw his body atop Amy McAslin and Krystal Goddard to shield them from the rifle fire. "Just truly incredible," McAslin later said, "a stranger, jumping over me to protect me."

The off-duty nurse from Orange County who told local news that she ran back into the danger to help the wounded: "I'm a nurse and I just felt that I had to ... There was so many people, just normal citizens, doctors, cops, paramedics, nurses, just off duty. ... It was completely horrible, but it was absolutely amazing to see all those people come together."

The anonymous man who threw 18-year-old Addison Short over his shoulder and carried her to safety. The couple who pulled their truck over to carry the wounded to the hospital. The off-duty police using their own bodies to cover the vulnerable. The father who protected his children from gunfire, saying, "They're 20. I'm 53. I lived a good life." Jonathan Smith, a 30-year-old who reportedly saved up to 30 lives, taking a bullet to the neck in the process.

It took hundreds of heroes to save hundreds of people; it took one evil man to wound and kill that many.

On the one hand, it is impossible not to lament the extent of evil: A man attacking those who harmed him in no way, possibly gleefully murdering people attending a concert, makes us wonder at the rot that can infect the human heart. But on the other hand, in each incident of horror we must remember how much the good outweighed the evil. Were there hundreds of people like Stephen Paddock, thousands would have died; were there only one person attempting to stop the impact of Paddock's evil, thousands would have died.

All of which means that as we mourn the victims in Las Vegas, we must also celebrate the heroes. We should see the incident as proof of just how much light infuses America from its citizens—how many normal people run to help each other when evil strikes, when darkness threatens to divide us. So long as that light continues to unite us, America will emerge ready, as always, to fight that darkness.

'Raising Awareness' Isn't Helping Much

October 18, 2017

"Awareness must be raised."

"A spotlight must be brought to this crucial issue."

"We must all think about our own culpability."

These tired nostrums are repeatedly deployed in our politics to explain why someone complains about a broad problem or tells a specific story of victimization without accompanying evidence that would allow us to act. Accusations of institutional racism rarely come along with specific allegations regarding specific police officers. If allegations and names were included, we could all look at the evidence and determine whether or not to call for consequences. Stories of sexual assault and harassment at work are often told without naming names. If those names were named, authorities could investigate; the media could begin collecting data; and we could do something about it.

But that would be useful. We don't want useful measures. We want to note how terrible things are generally.

Why?

What drives us to ignore the obvious fact that most Americans oppose specific evils and would side against those evils when presented with evidence of them occurring?

Perhaps it's our innate drive toward establishing a feeling of moral superiority. You don't get to feel morally superior when you name someone who acts in criminal fashion; you're just a witness, and witnesses are useful members of society, bettering society actively rather than criticizing it from the outside.

Or perhaps it's the burden that comes along with evidence. It's much easier to gain sympathy by telling a story about victimization without naming names—a story nobody can contradict, since you're not getting specific. In fact, if you *do* get too specific about allegations of sexual assault, as actress Lena Dunham did, your allegations might be called into question. And if you *do* get too specific about allegations of police racism and brutality, as the Seattle Seahawks defensive end Michael Bennett did, your accusations might be debunked.

So, is it worthwhile to complain about generalized problems without providing specific instances upon which we can agree and against which we can fight? Only on a marginal level—and in some ways, it's actually tremendously counterproductive. It may be useful to "raise awareness" among police officers about being careful in their procedures so as not to be accused of racism, for example. It may be useful to "raise awareness" among men in offices about being careful around female employees so as not to be accused of harassment. But it may also be counterproductive to rage against the system generally because it leads to false and widespread perceptions that *all* police officers are cursed with the original sin of racism, or that *all* men are cursed with "toxic masculinity."

So, here's an idea: Let's all call out bad action when we see it and be as specific as possible about it. We can all agree on what a bad guy looks like; there isn't much debate about Harvey Weinstein. But if we continue to promote the importance of "raising awareness" rather than providing evidence, our groundless distrust for one another is bound to grow and metastasize.

The Delusional Optimism of Both Sides

October 25, 2017

This week, President Trump went to battle with Gold Star widow Myeshia Johnson. Johnson's husband, Sgt. La David Johnson, was killed in Niger earlier this month. Trump called his widow to offer his condolences. But Myeshia Johnson apparently interpreted that call as a callously indifferent attempt to curry favor. She conveyed her displeasure to Rep. Frederica Wilson, D-Fla., who promptly went public with it. Trump responded to Johnson's anger not with compassion but with indignation: He stated that he had never been callous toward her.

The most likely explanation for this hubbub is misinterpretation on one or both sides. The chances that Trump wanted to offend Johnson are slim and none. But it's not politically or morally wise for Trump to begin a public firefight with a grieving widow.

So why are so many Republicans cheering him on? Because there are many on the right who believe that Trump simply cannot lose, that he has the political Midas touch. Their evidence: Trump said impolitic, offensive and boorish things regularly on the campaign trail in 2016, and he then won the election over Hillary Clinton.

Meanwhile, Democrats seem to believe that they need to offer no alternative to Trump's governing vision, that they can simply stand on the sidelines and scream at him. Thus, Sen. Sherrod Brown, D-Ohio, claims that Trump has staffed his White House with white supremacists; and Rep. Maxine Waters, D-Calif., says that she wants to "take out" Trump. Democrats' evidence for their obvious belief that Trump will certainly fall in 2020 is that Trump's approval ratings are abysmal and he lost the popular vote in 2016. Democrats see 2016 as a complete fluke.

Both sides, however, are wrong.

Trump supporters are wrong that Trump is untouchable. Trump didn't win in 2016 purely because he's some sort of Teflon candidate; he won because he ran against the weakest candidate in American history. Trump actually won fewer votes in Wisconsin than Republican nominee Mitt Romney did in 2012. Nobody showed up to vote for Clinton, so Trump won the state. Trump won fewer votes in Michigan than Republican nominee George W. Bush did in 2004. Nobody liked Clinton, so Trump won the state. What will happen if Democrats choose not to run a corrupt, venal and thoroughly charisma-free candidate? What will happen if they run former Vice President Joe Biden or Sen. Bernie Sanders? Between 2000, when George W. Bush lost the popular vote by about 544,000, and 2004, when he won it, he picked up some 10 million votes. Where is Trump going to pick up similar numbers?

Democrats are wrong that Trump will be a definite loser. Since 1968, just one elected incumbent president has lost re-election without a major third-party candidate in contention (President Jimmy Carter in 1980). Incumbency is a heavy advantage, and Democrats seem to be under the misimpression that they can continue to bank on the Obama coalition without President Obama on the ballot. They tried that with Clinton. It failed. In order to compete in the Rust Belt, Democrats need to leave behind intersectional identity politics. But that means alienating some of their base.

In the end, the calculus is simple: Trump can't afford to be cavalier, thinking he's guaranteed victory; Democrats can't afford to sit on their laurels and hope that Trump collapses. In any case, some cautious pessimism might be in order all the way around.

The Swamp Is D.C.

November 1, 2017

Get ready for a word problem.

Paul Manafort was Donald Trump's presidential campaign chairman. He allegedly had deep, long-lasting, corrupt ties to Russia for which he will likely go to prison if convicted—he's just been indicted by special counsel Robert Mueller. According to the indictment, he contracted with the Podesta Group—headed by Tony Podesta, a longtime Democratic lobbyist and brother of former Hillary Clinton campaign chairman John Podesta—to run interference for the Ukrainian government under now-deposed leader Viktor Yanukovych. Podesta stepped down from the group on Monday amid the Manafort allegations.

Meanwhile, former Trump campaign foreign policy adviser George Papadopoulos just pled guilty to lying to the FBI. He admits that he was attempting to connect with foreign sources with connections to the Russian government who promised a better Trump campaign-Russia relationship and stated they had "dirt" on Clinton, including "thousands of emails." Papadopoulos implicated other members of the campaign. This would be the second piece of evidence that someone in the Trump campaign was warm toward receiving information on Clinton via Russian sources. The first came earlier this year, when we found out that Donald Trump Jr. had openly encouraged a meeting with Russia-connected lawyers promising material on Clinton. Neither reach-out by the Russians apparently materialized into anything serious.

At the same time, we now know that Clinton's campaign paid Fusion GPS to fund an anti-Trump dossier compiled by one Christopher Steele, a former MI6 spy. Steele gathered information from Russian officials as well. This means that the Clinton campaign wasn't averse to gathering information from Russia to hurt Trump. And the FBI apparently founded a wiretap of a Trump associate on material in the Steele dossier. We don't know whether the charges in the Steele dossier were independently confirmed. But former FBI Director James Comey filled Trump in on them in January, while the FBI was interviewing Papadopoulos. And Trump fired Comey in May and then told Russian officials he had done so in order to relieve pressure on himself. Attorney General Jeff Sessions had already recused himself from Russian matters, which forced Deputy Attorney General Rod Rosenstein to consider recusing himself and appoint special counsel Robert Mueller, who had worked with Comey at the FBI.

So, here's the question: Who's guilty? Not of Russian interference but being terrible at the business of government.

The answer: Everyone.

President Trump was elected on the basis of a promise to "drain the swamp." But Trump was always part of the swamp. Of course, some of the swamp was of his own making—he has hung out in dicey circles his entire career. But some of it came from the Republican National Committee—Manafort was heavily connected there. And Clinton was part of the swamp for decades, too, which is why Trump's campaign manager was working with the brother of Clinton's campaign manager to push a pro-Russian agenda for years.

The American people saw the levels of corruption in Washington, D.C., and they responded by saying they wanted an outsider to clean things up. But things will never be clean so long as D.C. remains a central hoarding house for cash and power. The problem isn't Trump or Manafort or Podesta. The problem is that Washington, D.C., was never supposed to be this way, and that the flies have been drawn to the cesspool. If you want to "drain the swamp," you have to start with the institutions themselves, not with the people. The problem isn't having the worst people running the government; it's having the worst forms of government drawing the worst people.

What an American Hero Looks Like

November 8, 2017

This week, a discharged Air Force airman with a criminal record of domestic abuse, including cracking the skull of his infant stepson, stepped into a church in rural Texas and murdered 26 people, at least a dozen of them children. Americans broke out into their usual arguments over gun control and whether "thoughts and prayers" are helpful; we argued over politicizing tragedy and legislating away rights.

But each time an evil human being decides to attack innocents, it isn't the Twitter battles that stand between the monsters and children. It's heroes. It's men like Stephen Willeford.

In a vaccum, Willeford would be despised by the media. He's a former NRA instructor—you know, the National Rifle Association, a "domestic terror group" devoted to allowing bloodbaths, according to the left. He probably voted for President Trump. His family has lived in Sutherland Springs for four generations. He's parochial enough to attend church regularly. You know, he's a typical bitter clinger.

But when the gunman opened fire, it was Willeford who ran toward the danger. According to Willeford, his daughter told him someone had opened fire at the church half a block away from his home. Willeford immediately ran to his safe and removed his rifle, precisely the type of firearm so many on the left want to legislate out of existence. "I kept hearing the shots, one after another, very rapid shots," Willeford said later, "just 'Pop! Pop! Pop! Pop!' and I knew every one of those shots represented someone, that it was aimed at someone, that they weren't just random shots."

Willeford ran outside with his gun and loaded the magazine. He didn't even bother to put on shoes. And when he saw the piece of human debris responsible for the massacre, he opened fire. "I know I hit him," said Willeford. "He got into his vehicle, and he fired another couple rounds through his window."

The shooter sped away. Willeford hailed another vehicle, and he and the driver began chasing him. That's correct: Civilians chased a shooter through the streets and called 911 on the way. The shooter ended up crashing his car.

Willeford didn't pretend he wasn't afraid. He explained: "I was scared for me. I was scared for every one of them, and I was scared for my own family that just lived less than a block away. I am no hero. I am not. I think my God, my Lord, protected me and gave me the skills to do what needed to be done."

This humble man *is* an American hero. He's what America looks like: people in small towns; churchgoers who quietly raise families and make their communities better; people who have so much to lose because they've built so much without fanfare or reward; people who go running to help their neighbors when they must; men who run toward danger; men with the training and means necessary to stop bad men.

These people have always stood between good and evil. They always will. It won't be laws. It won't be regulations. Laws and regulations failed. Americans—innocent Americans—were murdered because of those failures. More would have died if not for the heroism of Stephen Willeford. Thank God for him.

What Are Our Representatives Supposed to Do?

November 15, 2017

During America's founding era, a significant debate took place about the nature of representation in a democratically elected government. Were representatives supposed to act as simple proxies for their constituents? Or were they supposed to exercise independent judgment? Edmund Burke was a forceful advocate for the latter position: A representative, he said, was supposed to exercise his "mature judgment, his enlightened conscience. And "he ought not to sacrifice to you, to any man, or to any set of men living." John Stuart Mill, too, believed that representatives ought to act independently; he said: "A person whose desires and impulses are his own...is said to have a character. One whose desires and impulses are not his own, has no character, no more than a steam-engine has a character."

Then there were those who argued that to exercise independent judgment would be to betray voters, that they sent you there with a mission, and your job is to fulfill that mission. This so-called delegate view of representation is supremely transactional—we only bother electing representatives in this view in order to do the work we're not willing to do. They aren't elected to spend time learning about the issues or broaden their perspective beyond the regional. They're there to do what you want them to do.

This debate has finally come to a head recently, not because sectional representatives have forgone their voters but because characterless people are running for office more and more. Those who believe in the Burkean model oppose such people—we say that to put those without character in charge of policy is to leave our future in the hands of the untrustworthy. Those who believe in the delegate model can embrace such people—they say that so long as the representative votes the right way on the issues, they can murder dogs in the backyard or allegedly molest young girls. Nina Burleigh's perspective on then-President Bill Clinton falls into this second camp. "I would be happy to give him a blow job just to thank him for keeping abortion legal," she said. So does Rep. Mo Brooks' perspective on Alabama Republican Senate candidate Roy Moore. He said: "Roy Moore will vote right ... That's why I'm voting for Roy Moore."

There's a certain freedom to this perspective. It allows us to forgo discussion about the nature of the people we support—so long as they're not lying about how they vote, we can trust them in office. The founders, however, would have rejected this perspective. The Federalist Papers are replete with explanations of just why a good government would require good men. The founders greatly feared the constraints of a parchment barrier against characterless men; they didn't trust human nature enough to believe that child molesters or puppy torturers would be bound by simple conformity with the public will.

And the founders were right. History has shown that bad men in positions of power rarely get better; they often get worse. They tend to abuse power. They tend to exercise their judgment—or lack thereof—even when they pledge to do otherwise. That means that we must measure our candidates for character as well as position. "May none but honest and wise men ever rule under this roof," President John Adams prayed regarding the White House. He didn't pray that they agree with him on tariffs.

The Sultans of America and Their Harems

November 22, 2017

Americans have been buried in the last six weeks by a blizzard of reports of sexual harassment, assault, misconduct and malfeasance from our politicians, journalists and Hollywood glitterati. In the last week alone, we've seen a picture of Sen. Al Franken, D-Minn., during his pre-senatorial days placing his hands over a sleeping woman's breasts; the suspension of New York Times journalist Glenn Thrush for allegedly harassing young female journalists; and eight women telling the Washington Post that fabled television host Charlie Rose had made unwanted sexual advances ranging from groping to lewd phone calls. That follows on the heels of allegations of child molestation against Alabama Senate Republican nominee Roy Moore, confirmed accusations of unwanted exposure from comedian Louis C.K. and allegations of sexual assault against Russell Simmons. Every day, it seems, a new member of the cultural aristocracy comes tumbling down.

What's behind all of it? Why did it take so long for this avalanche to start? And what does it tell us about the culture we've built?

Misconduct thrives when accountability fades. Historically speaking, we have always had elite classes of people who engaged in sexually atrocious behavior, and that class was largely confined to those with power and their hangers-on. Kings and potentates could revel in their harems—they could seize and rape concubines—and those upon whom they bestowed favor could expect to enjoy like treatment. But in an egalitarian, free society, a society without hereditary aristocracy, we pride ourselves on having a common standard of behavior for everyone.

That's simply not true. When it comes to sexual exploitation of women in particular, we treat our new aristocracy in the same way peasants treated the old aristocracy: with deference. In America, three things confer aristocratic status: fame, money and power. Hollywood, politics and journalism are built on all three. And elite status in each of those industries bought not just a bevy of opportunities for brutality but also a silent knowledge that the consequences would be slight for engaging in that brutality.

First, the opportunities. Just as certain peasants of old sought to curry favor with lords, too many Americans seek to curry favor with the powerful. That's the story of the Hollywood casting couch. It's the story of the famed journalist and his nighttime corner booth at the local pub. It's the story of the politician and his late-night office meetings. Does anyone think women were dying to meet Harvey Weinstein or Charlie Rose or Glenn Thrush? Each story we hear tells the same tale: Women thought the only way they could get ahead was to treat these men with complaisance. They thought that they couldn't turn down dinner invites. And if they were abused, they thought they had to keep their mouths shut.

In many cases, they did. That's because the public offered no consequences to the elite. Perhaps we blamed the victims and were unwilling to blame the accusers. Perhaps the darkest side of humanity revels in the pain inflicted by others. Whatever the case, the aristocrats knew, and they acted accordingly.

So, what's changed now? It's tempting to say that we've woken up—that we're unwilling to allow fame and money and power to excuse abuse, and we're not going to go back to the old way anymore. But that would be too sanguine. So long as fame and money and power exist, there will be those who seek to exploit them and those who look the other way. False idols always have their adherents.

It's our job to ensure that the idols remain smashed. And that means recanting our own idolatry for a cultural sultanate that deserves to be torn down.

Bill Clinton Won After All

November 29, 2017

Two weeks ago, it seemed that former President Bill Clinton was finished as a public figure. A variety of public intellectuals on the left had consigned him to the ashtray of history; they'd attested to their newfound faith in his rape accuser Juanita Broaddrick or torn him to shreds for having taken advantage of a young intern, Monica Lewinsky.

The moral goal was obvious: Set up a new intolerance for the sexual abuse of women. The political goal was even more obvious: Show that Democrats are morally superior to Republicans, and in doing so, shame Republicans into staying home rather than voting for Alabama Republican senatorial candidate Roy Moore, who has been credibly accused of sexual assault of minors.

Then it all fell apart.

On Sunday, House Minority Leader Nancy Pelosi, D-Calif.—the first female speaker of the House—brushed off Clinton's scandals with a simple one-liner: "Well, I think it's, obviously it is a generational change. But let me say the concern that we had then was that they were impeaching the president of the United States, and for something that had nothing to do with the performance of his duties."

Why would Pelosi defend Clinton? Because she also has to defend Sen. Al Franken, D-Minn., and Rep. John Conyers, D-Mich., both of whom have been accused of sexual harassment or sexual assault. And why would she have to defend either of them?

That's the $64,000 question. She really doesn't—just as the Democrats never had to defend Clinton. If they'd kept their mouths shut and let Clinton resign, then-Vice President Al Gore would have been president. There's a high likelihood he would have been re-elected in 2000. If the Democrats were to let Franken fall today, his replacement would be appointed by a Democratic governor of Minnesota. If they were to let Conyers go down, he'd be replaced in a special election in what The Cook Political Report deems a D+32 district, meaning it performed an average of 32 points more Democratic than the nation did as a whole in 2016. Democrats wouldn't miss a beat, and they'd have a shot at taking out Moore to boot. By defending Franken and Conyers, Democrats give Republicans ample opportunity to back Moore and point at Democratic hypocrisy all the while. While Republicans can at least point at the potential loss of a Senate seat to justify backing Moore, Democrats wouldn't suffer *any* loss by dumping Franken and Conyers.

There's only one real reason Pelosi would stand by accused Democrats: She doesn't care. Her logic with regard to Clinton is the only one that matters. He was a Democrat, and his sexual improprieties had nothing to do with his capacity for voting for her agenda. This was the national argument we had in 1998, and it was settled in Clinton's favor. Character doesn't matter. Only agenda does.

Republicans bucked that agenda. They don't anymore.

In order to shame Republicans, Democrats seemed to buck that agenda this time around. But that was all bluster.

Bill Clinton didn't just escape impeachment in 1998. He won the argument. He taught Americans that no matter how scummy our politicians might be, so long as they side with us on matters great or small, we ought to back them. We ought to back them not because our principles are important but because there might be some point in the future when our principles are at stake, and we don't want our feet held to the fire then, do we?

In the famous play "A Man for All Seasons," Sir Thomas More, betrayed by his former colleague Richard Rich in exchange for the post of attorney general in Wales, says: "Why, Richard, it profits a man nothing to give his soul for the whole world. ... But for Wales?" We're willing to give our souls for nothing. Or perhaps they're already gone.

Fiscal Responsibility or Lower Taxes?

December 6, 2017

This week, Republicans in the Senate finally passed their long-awaited tax reform plan. It lowers individual income tax rates across the board, although it does claw back some government revenue in the form of elimination of state and local tax deductions. It drops corporate tax rates as well. It is, in other words, a significant but not atypical Republican tax cut designed to boost economic growth by allowing Americans to keep more of their own money.

The tax cut will almost certainly increase the deficit, however. Even with dynamic scoring—the assumption that the economy will grow at a faster clip thanks to tax cuts—the tax cuts could lead to $1 trillion in lower revenue through 2027. This has led some conservatives to sour on tax reform altogether, rightly saying that Republicans were, until a few months ago, complaining incessantly about former President Obama's blowout deficits and the burgeoning national debt, which now stands at a cool $20.5 trillion. That doesn't include long-term unfunded liabilities, which are slated to bring the debt to some $70 to 75 trillion in coming decades.

So, which is more important: cutting deficits or cutting taxes?

The answer, in the long run, is obvious: cutting deficits. Deficits impoverish future generations; they undermine the credibility of our financial commitments; they prevent us from fulfilling promises we have already made to our own citizens. There are already millions of Americans who will never receive Social Security in the amount they have been promised; there are already millions of Americans unborn who will spend their lives paying off the commitments made by others for political gain.

At the same time, were we to raise taxes to pay off our debts, we would enervate our population and inure citizens to high taxes. Citizens of European states are used to insanely high tax rates; the impetus for spending cuts based on desire for lower taxes disappears after years of habituation to those tax rates and unsustainable government benefits. Europeans are used to the very social programs that continue to bankrupt them despite high tax rates; they're not clamoring to cut programs based on their distaste for those tax rates.

This puts American politicians in somewhat of a Catch-22. If they stump for spending cuts, they're cast as uncaring and cruel; if they stump for tax increases to pay for those spending cuts, they're cast as uncaring and cruel. Thus, the deficit continues to grow.

So, what should Republicans do about it? They ought to cut taxes, and then they ought to acknowledge that cuts are necessary to keep taxes low. Let Americans get used to keeping their own money. Let them understand that services aren't free. Then, be honest about the costs associated with big government programs.

In the end, both Democrats and Republicans will have to face a simple truth: It's either government cuts or bust. There's no reason for Republicans to give away their only leverage—the taste of the public for a dynamic economy based on individuals retaining their earnings—in order to shore up programs Democrats will only work to expand.

How to Deal With Bullies

December 13, 2017

This week, America found a new cause to rally around: Keaton Jones. Keaton is a middle school student who was apparently viciously bullied at school for the crime of having a scar on his head from the removal of a tumor. His mother filmed a video of him crying as he explained that other kids had poured milk over his head and mocked him; through his tears, Jones questioned why kids treat one another this way.

The video was absolutely heartbreaking.

It was particularly painful for me. I skipped two grades. By the time I hit sophomore year of high school, I was half a foot shorter and 40 pounds lighter than the other kids. The other kids had been in classes together for years; I was a newcomer. That meant being physically shoved into trash cans and lockers. On one overnight trip, some of my classmates handcuffed me to a metal-framed bed and then hit me repeatedly on the rear with a belt. I pretended to sleep through it, and rather unconvincingly.

So I know what Keaton went through. Being bullied makes you feel like a bottle about to burst—the frustration eats away at your stomach lining and makes you dread going to school. It makes you miserable; even when you're happy, you're constantly waiting for the next shoe to drop.

Still, I don't think Jones' mom should have taken that video.

I think that for two reasons. First, all the celebrity Jones has achieved here won't help him when the cameras turn off. The bullies will still be there, but they'll be twice as cruel, thanks to their belief that he has made fame and fortune off of them. They'll seek to justify their bad actions with more bad actions.

Second, Jones himself isn't going to be helped by this in the long term. No child should have to be bullied, and if someone ever tries to bully my kids, I'll step in with the full range of possibilities at my disposal. But being bullied can have two possible effects: You learn to stand up and cope, or you learn to identify as a victim. If you can hold your head up high even while you're being bullied, you're likely to live a stronger, happier, fuller life. That doesn't mean you're going to be able to knock out the bully a la Daniel in "The Karate Kid." But it does mean you'll be able to better deal with the vicissitudes life has to offer. Those won't end with middle school.

We worry—rightly—about bullying in schools. But we should also worry about how victims treat their victimhood and how they can turn that victimhood into strength for the long haul. Our society has sympathy for victims of bullying, as it should. But we should recognize that just as a wounded animal must be prepared to re-enter the wild lest it die in wild conditions, children must be prepared to live in wild conditions. Those conditions represent life for most people at most times. We can and should stick up for victims against bullies. But we should also focus on empowering victims to become the future bulwarks against bullying—for themselves and for their children.

Does Yes Ever Mean Yes?

December 20, 2017

Over the weekend, Jessica Bennett, gender editor of The New York Times—yes, that's a real title—wrote a piece titled "When Saying 'Yes' Is Easier Than Saying 'No'." She argued that in many cases, women say yes to sex but actually don't want to do so: "Sometimes 'yes' means 'no,' simply because it is easier to go through with it than explain our way out of the situation. Sometimes 'no' means 'yes,' because you actually *do* want to do it, but you know you're not *supposed to* lest you be labeled a slut. And if you're a man, that 'no' often means 'just try harder'—because, you know, persuasion is part of the game." Bennett continues by arguing that consent is actually societally defined, that "our idea of what we want—of our own desire—is linked to what we think we're *supposed* to want."

But Bennett offers no clear solutions to this issue. If it's true that women say yes but mean no, are men supposed to read minds? If a woman says no but a man seduces her until she says yes, is the initial no supposed to take precedence over the final yes?

Unfortunately, Bennett offers no guidance. Neither does Rebecca Reid, who wrote in Metro UK that she once participated in a threesome because she "didn't want to be rude." And Reid says that such experiences aren't uncommon: "There are hundreds of reasons why, but they all boil down to the same thing. We're nice girls. We've been raised to be nice." She adds: "sometimes being careful means having sex that you don't want, that leaves you feeling dirty and sad and a bit icky. It's not rape. It's not abuse. But it's not nice, either."

In the pages of The New Yorker, a similarly vague story went viral. Titled "Cat Person," it describes a woman named Margot who seduces a man and sends him all the signals that she wants to have sex with him but is internally divided over whether to go through with it: "she knew that her last chance of enjoying this encounter had disappeared, but that she would carry through with it until it was over." In the end, she cuts short their relationship, and he texts that she is a "Whore."

It's a painful story, to be sure. But it also raises a serious question: What exactly are men supposed to do in such scenarios? Because as a society, we're beyond suggesting that women are doing anything wrong in consenting to nonmarital sex; women are free to do what they want. But we *are* in the midst of a push to punish male aggressors. And if we water down consent to nothingness, how can we ever expect men to feel safe in the knowledge that a sexual encounter won't come with life-altering implications?

Perhaps the problem is expectations. All three articles articulate the complaint that women want to fulfill men's expectations. But none of them admit to another expectation, one created by the feminist movement: the expectation that women themselves must treat sex casually or fall prey to reinforcing the patriarchy. Ask a person of traditional moral standards whether the woman should have said no in all of these stories. The answer will be yes. But then that person will be regarded as a prude.

There are costs to societal expectations. Traditional mores ruled out the male expectation of sex in non-commitment scenarios. Yes, men had hopes of sex—all men do, virtually all of the time. But men had no expectation that such hopes would be achieved absent serious commitment. Thanks to our consent-only society, however, in which sexual activity is a throwaway and any notion of cherishing it is scoffed at as patriarchal, men have developed expectations that too many women feel they must meet—and men have taken up the feminist standard that consent is a goal to be achieved. The cost to such a system is borne almost entirely by women.

The healthiest system of sexual interaction is a system in which most women can be sure enough of themselves most of the time to feel decent after saying yes. That system no longer exists, thanks to the disconnect between commitment and sex. And the continuing disconnect between consent and expectation will continue to burden women in heavier and heavier ways.

Time to Defund the United Nations

December 27, 2017

Last week, Democrats and many in the mainstream media became highly perturbed by the Trump administration's suggestion that the United States might tie continued foreign aid to support for its agenda abroad. Foreign dictators agreed. Turkish President Recep Tayyip Erdogan, who spent the last year arresting dissidents, announced, "Mr. Trump, you cannot buy Turkey's democratic free will with your dollars, our decision is clear."

Herein lies the great irony of the United Nations: While it's the Mos Eisley of international politics—a hive of scum and villainy—and it votes repeatedly to condemn the United States and Israel, the tyrannies that constitute the body continue to oppress their own peoples. Among those who voted last week to condemn the U.S. for recognizing Jerusalem as Israel's capital and moving its embassy to Jerusalem were North Korea, Iran, Yemen and Venezuela. Why exactly should the United States *ever* take advice from those nations seriously?

We shouldn't. And we should stop sending cash to an organization that operates as a front for immoral agenda items.

The United Nations spends the vast majority of its time condemning Israel: According to UN Watch, the U.N. Human Rights Council issued 135 resolutions from June 2006 to June 2016, 68 of which were against Israel; the U.N. Educational, Scientific and Cultural Organization *only* passes resolutions against Israel; and the U.N. General Assembly issued 97 resolutions from 2012 through 2015, 83 of which targeted Israel.

Meanwhile, the U.N. has done nearly nothing with regard to Syria. It has instead suggested that Israel turn over the Golan Heights to the Syrian regime. The U.N. can't even successfully prevent the slaughter of the Rohingya in Myanmar. But they certainly have something say about whether the United States ought to recognize Jerusalem as Israel's capital.

One of the great lies of the Obama administration was that diplomacy is a foreign policy. We often heard from it that the only two alternatives were diplomacy and war. That was the stated reason for pursuing a one-sided nuclear deal with Iran that left Iran with burgeoning regional power and legitimacy. "What? Do you want a war or something?" it asked.

But the moment that the Trump administration uses tools of diplomacy, including financial pressure, to achieve American ends, the left complains. Would it prefer war? Diplomacy is a tool, not a foreign policy, and the use of diplomacy to pressure other nations to follow our lead is not only smart but also necessary. That is why the Trump administration was exactly right to negotiate a $285 million cut to the U.N.'s budget. Now we ought to slash our contributions to the counterproductive organization, since we pay one-fifth of the total bill.

The U.N. has always been a foolish fantasy, a League of Nations knockoff that's been about as productive and twice as irritating. It's an outmoded organization that's outlived whatever small usefulness it once had. There's no reason for us to continue cutting checks to prop up regimes that condemn us publicly for exercising the most basic standards of morality.

About the Author

Ben Shapiro was born in 1984. He entered the University of California Los Angeles at the age of 16 and graduated summa cum laude and Phi Beta Kappa in June 2004 with a Bachelor of Arts degree in Political Science. He graduated Harvard Law School cum laude in June 2007.

Shapiro was hired by Creators Syndicate at age 17 to become the youngest nationally syndicated columnist in the United States. His columns are printed in major newspapers and websites including *The Riverside Press-Enterprise* and the *Conservative Chronicle*, Townhall.com, ABCNews.com, WorldNetDaily.com, Human Events, FrontPageMag.com, and FamilySecurityMatters.com. His columns have appeared in *The Christian Science Monitor, Chicago Sun-Times, Orlando Sentinel, The Honolulu Advertiser, The Arizona Republic, Claremont Review of Books,* and RealClearPolitics.com. He has been the subject of articles by *The Wall Street Journal, The New York Times,* The Associated Press, and *The Christian Science Monitor.* He has been quoted on "The Rush Limbaugh Show" and "The Dr. Laura Show," at CBSNews.com, and in the *New York Press, The Washington Times,* and *The American Conservative.*

Shapiro is the author of best-sellers *Brainwashed: How Universities Indoctrinate America's Youth, Porn Generation: How Social Liberalism Is Corrupting Our Future,* and *Project President: Bad Hair and Botox on the Road to the White House.* He has appeared on hundreds of television and radio shows around the nation, including *The O'Reilly Factor, Fox and Friends, In the Money, DaySide with Linda Vester, Scarborough Country, The Dennis Miller Show, Fox News Live, Glenn Beck Show, Your World with Neil Cavuto, 700 Club, The Laura Ingraham Show, The Michael Medved Show, The G. Gordon Liddy Show, The Rusty Humphries Show, "The Lars Larson Show, The Larry Elder Show, The Hugh Hewitt Show,* and *The Dennis Prager Show.*

Shapiro is married and runs Benjamin Shapiro Legal Consulting in Los Angeles.

D.C.'S DIRTY POLITICS
is also available as an e-book
for Kindle, Amazon Fire, iPad, Nook and
Android e-readers. Visit
creatorspublishing.com to learn more.

∘ ∘ ∘

CREATORS PUBLISHING

We publish books.
We find compelling storytellers and
help them craft their narrative,
distributing their novels and collections
worldwide.

∘ ∘ ∘

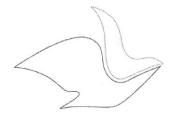

Made in the USA
Columbia, SC
22 September 2019